"What a strange and wonderful combination of experience and expertise. Mark Petersen, former missionary in the developing world with a spiritual care and leadership focus, and son of entrepreneurial parents with a passion for philanthropy, ends up as the director of the private family foundation that gives away multi-millions for social good, on two separate occasions walks The Camino across Spain, and then births a book that blends it all together with poignant observations, winsome stories, and an intoxicating passion. In a culture that is confused about whether to follow heroes or succumb to the democratization of everything, this book offers the image of the faith-filled pilgrim plodding through the bumpy world of philanthropy with an incisive clarity. A gift."

—ROD WILSON
Consultant; Pastor; former President, Regent College, Vancouver, Canada

"Mark Petersen has thoughtfully, reflectively, prayerfully walked The Camino as a pilgrim. He has also actively participated thoughtfully, reflectively, prayerfully with charities in their work of making a difference in the world which is God's world. To read about either of these journeys of faith would be a privilege and a gift but to read how Mark has intertwined them in word, action, and life is a blessing and the setting of an authentic path for us all. In this very creative book, the story of Camino journeys is brought together with the story of the Bridgeway family foundation and both their clearly articulated priorities for the funds that they share and their learnings along the donor journey. With an emphasis on capacity-building and innovation and the nurturing of the ability to see opportunities to inject creative capital into a charity at a particular moment in its history, Mark Petersen has written a very valuable book for donors and charities and those who recognize the joy and the Gospel imperative to give from what we have received. A 'Buen Camino' of Life to us all!"

—KAREN HAMILTON
General Secretary, The Canadian Council of Churches

"This book is desperately needed within the places where donor fundraising and philanthropy intersect. In *Love Giving Well* Mark Petersen moves beyond the transactional to the journey of giving and receiving in which partnership and growth is nurtured. He puts a face on the donor and receiver calling for a new way of relating. It is not easy but Mark knows what he is talking about. He has lived it. This book is a must-read for anyone working in the area of fundraising and those whose generosity is mirrored in their philanthropic endeavors."

—GARY NELSON
President and Vice Chancellor, Tyndale University College & Seminary

Love Giving Well

Ryan & Cindy

Thank you for opening
your home & your hearts
and for welcoming
Opportunity in!
Wonderful part of
the story
With Joy
Doris Clefrie

Love Giving Well

The Pilgrimage of Philanthropy

MARK PETERSEN

Foreword by
LORNA DUECK

 CASCADE *Books* · Eugene, Oregon

LOVE GIVING WELL
The Pilgrimage of Philanthropy

Cascade Books
An Imprint of Wipf and Stock Publishers
199 W. 8th Ave., Suite 3
Eugene, OR 97401

www.wipfandstock.com

PAPERBACK ISBN: 978-1-5326-0186-6
HARDCOVER ISBN: 978-1-5326-0188-0
EBOOK ISBN: 978-1-5326-0187-3

Cataloguing-in-Publication data:

Names: Petersen, Mark.

Title: Love giving well : the pilgrimage of philanthropy / Mark Petersen.

Description: Eugene, OR: Cascade Books, 2017 | Includes bibliographical references.

Identifiers: ISBN 978-1-5326-0186-6 (paperback) | ISBN 978-1-5326-0188-0 (hardcover) | ISBN 978-1-5326-0187-3 (ebook)

Subjects: LCSH: 1. Charity. | 2. Charities. | 3. Humanitarianism. | I. Title.

Classification: HV40.35 P45 2017 (paperback) | HV40.35 (ebook)

Manufactured in the U.S.A.   03/14/17

Poem by Luci Shaw used by permission.

For Karen, who lives and loves generously

I am a pilgrim, but my pilgrimage has been wandering and unmarked. Often what has looked like a straight line to me has been a circling or a doubling back.

. . .

I am an ignorant pilgrim, crossing a dark valley. And yet for a long time, looking back, I have been unable to shake off the feeling that I have been led – make of that what you will."

–Wendell Berry[1]

1. Berry, *Jayber Crow*, 133.

Contents

Attitudes

Transformation

Foreword

By Lorna Dueck

I like to introduce Mark as my friend who walked across Spain, twice. Surely there is enough curiosity in that odd trek to make one have to explain why. And how exactly does one cross a country on foot? Nearly as odd is the task of giving away money, rather than keeping and consuming it, and Mark has that journey in his story as well. I've known this man and his passion for strategic giving for fifteen years now, and more than anyone I know, he understands the enduring journey of making the world a better place.

When Jesus commissioned his followers, he told them to look for people like my friend. These charitable workers were not sent with a bag of money for their tasks, rather, there were told to look for welcome. "Whatever town or village you enter, search there for some worthy person and stay at their house until you leave,"[1] said Jesus.

I've been in Mark's "house" for all of my leadership journey of working with media and the gospel, and I'm so thankful for the "worthy person" he, his extended family and Bridgeway Foundation have been. They are a philanthropy community that has given out welcome, not just money—but also friendship, counsel, cheer, and a host of worthy ideas and qualities. As I read *Love Giving Well*, I recognized years of his beliefs, learnings, and developments shared in these pages.

You'll discover why strategy in giving helps you become better connected to your purpose; in fact, this book itself is evidence of Mark's conviction that being a strategist moves one along a continuum for being fruitful with our lives. It's realistic to learn that it hasn't been a smooth journey; it's okay that, as Mark puts it, his work is "slow, incremental, and painfully complicated."

1. Matt 10:11, NIV.

You'll learn that charity leaders aren't the only ones who make mistakes, philanthropists do also. Mark reveals, as only an insider can, the confusion, emotion, and even loneliness that comes with having money. This book moves givers from sentimental response, to intelligent inquiry methods and assessment planning. It covers logistics like conditional granting and dashboard indicators. It even explains a phrase I wondered years ago if Mark had invented: "capacity building."

When our charity was new and bursting with conquests to tackle, Mark pushed back a grant request and said, "Let's talk about capacity building instead." To pull back the curtain just a bit more here, Mark's wife, Karen, was also a volunteer in our fledgling charity, and frankly, he had a short cut to his rather rigorous assessment process in the pillow talk they likely shared. The honesty and candor he brought back to me in that moment of learning is in these pages too. He taught me that building my charity's capacity is core to my work as a leader, which has remained a lifelong lesson.

In these chapters you will learn what a difference that phrase, *capacity building*, can make in the pilgrimage of bringing hope and healing, and what a health-giving, protective process capacity building can be for nonprofit work and their philanthropic investors. Being teachers as they gave was one of the reasons Bridgeway Foundation became known among charity leaders as the blue ribbon seal for maturity in organizational process. Maturity does not mean perfection, rather, it came to be known that if you could receive a gift from Bridgeway and make its reporting and results standards, there was a depth in an organization that would help it weather the storms that charity life can bring. With this book, Mark shares what he and his family learned in those many years of crafting such a reputation in philanthropy.

Wealth whispers. Precisely because of that reality, because of the virtues of modesty and humility and because of the need for privacy that accompany people of wealth, these chapters are a gold mine of insight into issues that are seldom discussed. Over the years, Mark has pulled the whispers of wealth into open dialogue. It's been part of the philosophy he teaches in these pages, on helping others know their parameters and being able to say, with confidence, a no or yes to opportunities. It's coaching, plain and simple, in how to communicate in the sensitive world of philanthropy, how to speak the negatives, how to celebrate the positives, and how to persist in the winding road to success.

Foreword

We are apparently living in times of the largest wealth transfer ever, an astonishing thirty trillion dollars will move from generous and hardworking boomers to millennials. Surely a talk about how to handle our wealth and sharing it with those who truly need it is part of our collective pilgrimage for these times. It likely took both of those long walks all across Spain for these ideas to coalesce in this book, but I'm glad they did. We will be richer as a result.

Introduction

Pilgrimage is not the first metaphor one thinks of when considering philanthropy. But having engaged in both, I've had ample time to consider the parallels. In the summers of 2014 and 2015, I had the transformative experience of walking across Spain on what's called the Camino, following the footsteps of hundreds of thousands who have walked those same paths since medieval times.

Over those month-long journeys, I contemplated how my own evolution in philanthropy has had much in common with the experience of pilgrimage.

For fifteen years, I had the responsibility of running a Canadian foundation. We took risks, created new patterns of engagement, pioneered new forms of collaboration, and contributed to meaningful investment for changed lives in Canada and abroad. Over this period, we invested over $35 million of private wealth into social good. Today, I am building on this experience to launch a new platform for giving by major donors, one that emphasizes collaboration and strategy.

But that speaks more of my destination. To explain how I got here, I need to back up. It's been more than a trip, larger than a journey. It has been a pilgrimage.

As a philanthropist, I have learned while walking along the pathway of generosity. My walking has not been straightforward; I've bumbled along, discovering along the way what makes for good giving. I don't have a finance degree. I didn't make the money that is entrusted to me. But, unexpectedly, I was given stewardship responsibilities for wealth that was destined to be invested strategically into charitable activity.

Likewise, in my physical journey, I learned lessons while walking to Santiago de Compostela, the cathedral city in Galicia, northwestern Spain, where the remains of the Apostle James are said to be interred.

Legend says that one of the Sons of Thunder, James the Greater, was the apostle who took the good news to the Iberian Peninsula following the death and resurrection of Christ. On his return to Jerusalem in 44 AD, however, he was slain by those who opposed the burgeoning and controversial Christian movement. His followers took his body back to Spain for burial, and tradition claims his boat was blanketed with scallop shells upon arrival.

James's remains were interred in a field, and, during the centuries of the Moorish caliphate in Spain, were forgotten. They were rediscovered in the 850s by a farmer. As word spread, that field was built up into the city of Santiago de Compostela. King Alfonso II the Chaste from Asturias, a neighboring principality, started the tradition of pilgrimage in earnest in the 900s by walking from Oviedo to Santiago to pay homage to James—the first of the many Caminos (or Ways) that now crisscross Europe. By medieval times during Christian Spain's ascendency, hundreds of thousands of pilgrims made the journey that could begin anywhere in Europe. Pilgrims eventually coalesced along various pathways leading to Santiago: the Camino Primitivo, the Camino Francés, the Camino del Norte, and the Vía de la Plata, among others. The scallop shell is the unifying symbol between Camino routes: as scallop shells have many grooves leading to a singular point, each of these Caminos led to one destination.

The journey could take months, even years, for medieval pilgrims. (And then they had to turn around to walk home!) Depictions of pilgrims portray them with a staff to aid in walking, a gourd for drinking water and wine, and a bag for any possessions. Often they would wear a scallop shell to indicate they were pilgrims on a journey to Santiago, and as a result were able to lodge in *hospitales,* or hostels, which aided them in curing their sores and attended to basic needs of food, drink, rest, and community.

In the past twenty years, the Camino pilgrimages have revived in popularity, especially among European youth, most of whom walk without deep reference to the Christian tradition behind this journey. Yet anyone who believes western spirituality is stagnant needs only to walk the Camino with Italian, German, French, and Spanish youth who are cultivating an unconventional yet living spiritual sensitivity and rejuvenated respect for their historical faith.

My two journeys were not as arduous, but neither were they walks in the park. In the summer of 2014, I started in St-Jean-Pied-de-Port, a Basque town in southeastern France at the foot of the Pyrenees, and walked with my younger son, Nate, some 800 kilometers over the Pyrenees into Spain, through the vineyards of Navarra and Rioja, across the heat and plains of the Meseta, and up and into the verdant, living mountains of Celtic Galicia. My wife, Karen, joined us in León to walk the last 300 kilometers—a dramatic feat in and of itself.

A year later I resurrected my backpack from its dark corner in my closet, and attempted the second journey alone. My second Camino was also around 800 kilometers and followed the difficult northern coastal route of the Camino del Norte from Irún on the French border, through Basque Country, Cantabria, and Asturias, then hooked south to Oviedo on the Camino Primitivo to trace the journey of Alfonso II to the cathedral city.

Each journey took slightly more than a month, and I averaged twenty-five kilometers per day. I usually stayed in hostels, ate communal meals with fellow pilgrims, and slept in bunk beds with a dozen or more snorers sharing the space. Walking was not easy, especially on the second journey where there often were great ascents and descents each day, and where villages with available hostel beds were often located at the verge of one's physical capability.

These journeys pushed me to my limit. They made me question why I had even begun, and allured me with fantasies of giving up. Close living with dozens of others at times had me questioning my sanity. Language barriers were frequent, and we were often reduced to childish gesturing to communicate. The smells, cultural practices, various religious beliefs, heat, rain, snoring, bedbugs, poorly made bunk beds, and complete and utter exhaustion all contributed to challenging one's pilgrimage.

I began to link pilgrimage with philanthropy after seeing similarities between the two. Throughout this book, I will encourage you to do the same. Although my Camino pilgrimages were spiritual experiences for me as a Christian, I believe that, just as many of my fellow pilgrims did not share my faith, readers of this book will be able to fully enjoy the journey regardless of their own beliefs about spiritual matters. I won't hide my own faith perspective, but I also won't make you feel less than welcome. I believe we can walk together on this journey and learn from one another.

Though you begin alone, an incredibly diverse community begins to form as a group of completely unrelated people begin walking over many weeks. Soon a solo walk evolves into a community walk centered on one goal. My original goal was solitude: I began craving simplicity, contemplation, and freedom from the clutter of my busy life. I ended together with new friends who mutually buoyed one another up, and was propelled forward by vastly different individuals who surrendered their own agendas to focus on the common goal. What drew us together was shared humanity despite fundamental differences, focused on the simplicity of a journey forward and the final destination. In our chaotic world, we often focus on what divides us. We feel threatened by our competition. We forget we are often moving in the same direction.

Pilgrimage challenges us to discard all the excess baggage that is unnecessary for the journey and that weighs us down: that extra pair of pants, the book that won't get read, oversized ointments and creams that can be purchased or borrowed if needed. As we journey on the road of philanthropy, we learn that to end well we must also give up things that are hard to relinquish: an ego that seeks being at the center, and a go-it-alone self-sufficiency that impoverishes with isolation and limited resources. We learn to ask for help. We share information on the next lodging available. We grow in suffering with others. We share food and water. We give each other a hand when about to fall. We abandon all thought of moving forward alone on the journey.

A walking pilgrimage means going slowly. There is no need to rush, or to be consumed by the urgency that normally guides our decisions. We stop to drink in mountain vistas, or eat a picnic together on the side of the path. We drill down to the basics: washing clothes by hand, letting them dry in the sun, or dangling them from our backpacks the following day if still damp. We learn to listen to nature's rhythms of wind and rain, sunrise and dusk. We learn to pay attention to each other's stories as we walk step by step. Going on pilgrimage teaches you to be human again.

As you walk, you gather companions and have conversations with people with whom would never normally relate—flung together only because you're moving in the same direction. Some of these relationships become foundational to your journey, and you decide to walk daily together. Other connections are brief, each depending on the pace of the pilgrim, her priorities, or his physical capability.

Likewise, some philanthropists have already begun the journey of reorganizing their lives away from materialistic accumulation. They have recognized that extreme financial wealth is not necessary for life, and they see good in sharing it for charitable purposes. In this decision, they have made the first steps of pilgrimage: walking without all that extra stuff. But there are many other things to dispose of along the way, and an even greater number of things to gain in this shared journey.

As philanthropists, we usually begin by walking alone: we are shy to broadcast our generous intentions, and giving is considered a solo pursuit. But when we lift our gaze, we perceive there are others ahead to learn from, and that, if we pause to rest, others behind can catch up to us. Like pilgrims on the Camino, we need to travel together. Hopefully the philanthropist can learn to enjoy the journey with others rather than remain alone, overwhelmed by relentless demands and expectations.

Like pilgrimage, philanthropy is also a slow journey. You don't see change overnight. You take step after step after step. Short cuts can work, but often turn out badly. Patience is required. You must know the tilt of the land, the rocks along the way, and the weather patterns that affect your walking forward.

In my experience, people who have great capacity to give face various emotions. Some are completely paralyzed by the task before them, trapped by the fear of making a mistake. Others have been burned by repeated pestering from organizations who want to woo them, and they give begrudgingly. I've seen others motivated by guilt, and the resulting gift is given rashly, carelessly, like throwing a monkey off one's back. I've given in each of these ways as giving is not the easy task that many believe it to be. It's my hope, therefore, that this book will be of assistance to all who yearn to give well, but who find the whole giving business paralyzing, perplexing, or guilt-inducing.

This book is not just a message from one foundation executive to other wealthy givers. Institutional givers, such as churches, denominations, and corporate donation programs can benefit from this book's ideas. However, it's likely that the majority of readers will *not* have significant discretionary wealth to speak of. Many readers may have careers in the nonprofit sector—as CEOs, development directors, senior leadership, program staff—and will be intrigued to discover thoughts from someone involved in making decisions about grants. Most of us are inclined to give, and many orient our lives toward generosity.

In the following pages, I will detail what I have learned from leading a mid-sized, family-based philanthropic organization, the changes we have experienced on this journey, and some of the best practices we have cultivated. In my fifteen years in this role, we have attempted to model transparent, accessible philanthropy. This clarity has come from investing time and thoughtfulness into determining our core strengths and opportunities. It has allowed us the ability to say no gracefully and firmly. We are grateful to be able to say yes with enthusiasm and joy. We have become dedicated partners on the journey with nonprofit leaders who have challenged the way we think and live.

In this journey, over time I've evolved and priorities have changed, abandoning some perspectives and acquiring others as I advance on my philanthropy pilgrimage. Each person's journey is unique to them, and my walk of philanthropy will be different from most others. I believe that sharing what I have learned on the way will be beneficial, even if only to contrast it with others' journeys and to offer grantmakers an opportunity to reflect intentionally on their own philanthropic dreams and experiences in giving.

As we move along, I'll introduce conventional wisdom that is common among philanthropists. Many of these attitudes and practices, if adopted unthinkingly, can become traps. For a richer, more robust, and joyful philanthropy, it's necessary to move beyond these common pitfalls. We naively start off our journeys full of good intentions, but encounter thorny briars such as the failure to communicate clearly and set thoughtful strategy. Large donations can often create unnecessary potholes for those behind us on the path. Giving with strings attached or to exert undue or unrecognized power generates thunderous storm clouds that darken the day—when lightning strikes, someone can get burned. Hiding behind barriers and playing hard to get are like the nasty blisters that form on a pilgrim's heel and toe.

Many philanthropists are farther along on this journey than I am. Others have legitimate reasons to select alternative pathways that embrace some of the concepts I am moving away from. Philanthropy is indeed an intensely personal journey (albeit with public implications), but there are many ways to walk towards our destination.

Because my physical pilgrimage across the coastline and mountains of Spain is a metaphor for the arduous, yet joyous, journey of philanthropy, I begin each chapter with journal entries from my 2015 Camino walk along the Camino del Norte and Camino Primitivo. My diary introduces a taste of my physical and psychological journey across Spain, but it is also intended to root the reader in the forward motion that is needed by all of us to enjoy a transformational philanthropy.

At the end of each chapter I will include some thoughts for discussion and suggest resources that can be used by individuals and families on the journey of philanthropy. One of the biggest pitfalls in family philanthropy is the lack of communication about what drives us forward. I invite you to use these simple questions as jumping-off points for discussion with your loved ones.

In your philanthropy journey, heave up your backpack, take a deep breath, and let's move forward together, step by step. *¡Buen Camino!*

Beginnings

The tide that outward ebbs, turns then and inward flows
And what I offer you, you'll multiply to me.

−LUCI SHAW[1]

---

1. Shaw, "The Returns of Love," in *Harvesting Fog*, 17.

1

Surprised by philanthropy

Irún (Day 0)

My plane landed in Madrid, and I linked up with Rosa, a friend from last year's walk across Spain. Rosa and her husband, Jorge, natives of the Spanish capital, picked me up at the airport and I threw my thirty-eight-liter backpack, compact iPad bag, and hat into the trunk of their Fiat. We had lunch, then parked at the cathedral and did the tourist thing—walking and talking about the downtown core, the Royal Palace, and the Mercado de San Miguel. When they dropped me off at my lodging for the night, we opened the trunk which was curiously emptied of my iPad bag, and, strangely, my hat. We determined we must have been robbed while parked at the cathedral.

That hat had emotional value. I had worn it every day last year when I walked the Camino Francés with my son Nate. We had started that camino in the French town of St-Jean-Pied-de-Port, and hiked over the Pyrenees on our first day. Violent winds wanted to seize that hat and I literally had to tie it to my chin to keep it on as we crested the stark summit. It protected me through the intense heat and monotony of the bone-dry, flat meseta weeks later; it was respectfully removed in every church I visited; and it crowned me as we arrived in Santiago after thirty-three days of difficult walking.

The iPad had value also. But an evening trip to the Madrid Apple store in the center solved that problem—oh, the wonders of globalization and insurance! Perhaps it would take more to strip me of my security. The iPad, its contents backed up in the cloud, had earlier drafts of this book. During this second camino I hoped for time and space to focus again on it.

Beginnings

After an early double espresso and croissant at Madrid's Chamartin Station, I boarded a train and by midday arrived in Irún—a border town at the extreme northeastern edge of the country where Spain, France, and the Atlantic Ocean meet. I found the albergue or hostel—a plain, cramped apartment which opened every afternoon to receive a new round of pilgrims. Upon arrival, I received a message from Basque friends, Edurne Mujika and her husband Alberto, who lived in nearby San Sebastián. We had also walked the camino together last year. Tonight was their only evening available to meet, so I dropped off my backpack at the albergue and, feeling strangely free, hopped on a commuter train for the twenty-minute ride to meet them for dinner.

Despite my pilgrim wanderings, life continued to happen all around those who walk the camino. Alberto is a banker, and a member of a Basque association called a sociedad. Historically these were men's-only clubs which gave the group access to a fantastic downtown location on the harbor for hospitality. Fortunately, women are now permitted, but only the men were allowed in the kitchen to cook. After standing and socializing at a few crowded pinxtos, or tapas bars, and meeting some of their friends, we assembled in the sociedad where Alberto prepared us a meal: fresh tomato salad drizzled with olive oil and coarse sea salt, white asparagus spears, beef seared on the outside with a rosy red center, and crusty French baguettes. As is Basque tradition, he made quite a production of his cider-pouring two feet above the glass. Following the custom, we looked into each other's eyes and, in unison, drank the one inch of cider in a single swallow.

Alberto and Edurne drove me back to Irún long past midnight. In most albergues there is a strict locked-door policy after ten, but Ester, the hospitalera, had snuck me a key and suggested the bed by the door. I crept in and was quickly asleep on a bottom bunk. Tomorrow I would start my pilgrimage towards Santiago along the Camino del Norte.

As I settled into my bunk that night, my mind went back to a day eighteen years earlier when I was inducted into a journey of philanthropy. It began as a surprise. I began walking this new path in the town of Batangas, Philippines. The details of that morning were still fresh in my mind.

The rising humidity from the early morning sun had predicted another energy-depleting Filipino day as I trudged home from our neighborhood bakery with a dozen *pandesal* for my family. The buns, hot from the oven, heated the bag and left butter smudges on the plain brown paper. My flip-flops sounded a rhythmic *thwack-thwack-thwack* as I walked. Dust filled the air, particles suspended, glistening, dancing in the morning light as jeepneys roared past with early commuters.

After a few blocks, I turned into our townhouse—a simple 400-square-foot rental unit, sufficient for my wife, Karen, and I, and our two school-aged sons. Even this unassuming residence was a target in a nation where we lived better than most—it was clad with iron bars over the windows, and I had to work my way through a gate and two locks to enter my home.

Quietly so as not to disturb my sleeping family, I continued the morning routine. I filled a pot with purified water from the jug delivered last week, lit the burner with a match, and scooped coffee from the plastic canister. All our pantry items were sealed in Tupperware to protect from the geckos and roaches, or worse, that cat-sized rat that had the savvy to scamper out to terrify Karen when I was out.

I had snuck a still-warm piece of *pandesal* into my mouth when the shrill ring of the phone interrupted. The line crackled and hiccupped, alerting me that the call was from overseas. My dad's warm tone assured me this was not an emergency. In that moment, I didn't realize that this unexpected call would radically alter our lives. He announced that the family business, into which he had poured twenty years of his life, had just been sold to one of Canada's most prominent entrepreneurial families after a challenging series of negotiations.

Back in the early 1980s, when my parents' nursing home company began to grow quickly, my parents, Reg and Carol Petersen, had set the stage for what would become Bridgeway Foundation. Against the advice of their lawyers and accountants, and the prevailing materialistic culture that urged them to keep accumulating more, they chose to freeze their estate, and put all future company profits into a foundation with assets to be used for charitable purposes. For the next two decades while their company was expanding aggressively, it required all extra resources to be ploughed back into it. During that time, their foundation existed on paper, unendowed, waiting for the eventual sale of the company. The dream was to one day be able to give generously through an endowed foundation to charitable causes and local community activities.

With this unexpected sale of the company, instantly millions of dollars endowed our foundation.

The conversation with my dad was surreal as I was surrounded by the simplicity and poverty of daily Filipino life. This was where we hung our laundry out to dry, where electrical "brownouts" were a daily occurrence, where the four of us squeezed together on my dirt bike to go to church or the market, where we visited families in the *barangays* and shared simple stories of faith. I hung up, and forced the news out of my mind—it was too distant, too foreign to my experience—and went back to the work of serving the poor in a tropical island nation.

But that critical phone call was a turning point in my life. In one sense, I had already pursued a career in philanthropy. Mine wasn't philanthropy of money, but of action and presence. For ten years, I had invested my life into serving the poor and seeing people raised up through teaching, mentoring, and humanitarian service in poor contexts around the world. Pouring time and energy into serving others allowed for expressions of philanthropy that aren't typically considered. It colored how I would engage with others as I evolved to manage a multimillion-dollar foundation, and assisted other wealthy donors in deploying their resources for the common good.

On that day, my philanthropy broadened to also include monetary giving through Bridgeway Foundation, and on that journey, I have learned much which can be applied to anyone with a heart to give. Whether one gives $20 or $200,000, volunteers an hour or a lifetime, giving can be—and should be—much more than a transaction. It can be the moment for personal transformation, for realignment of priorities, a humbling process of grace. It is an opportunity to join with others, to drop barriers imposed by wealth and social status, to discover the beauty of the human family and the face of God at work in our world.

Many people who give consider their donation to be a mere financial transaction. As givers, we often engage from safe distances that really don't allow us the opportunity of being transformed by the complex realities of social need. Our gifts are delivered as one-off payouts driven by a vague sense that maybe our money can make a difference. But boiling our philanthropy down to transactions of cash will lead us to miss the fundamental transformational opportunity that exists for donors of all capacities.

Transformation can occur in a giver only when we open up to the opportunity, and in a meaningful way unique to each person, engage in the work of the organizations we support.

Giving is about much more than financial transactions. Engaged generosity has the potential to radically transform our way of life and attitudes towards living. When you come close to need, your heart can be broken and expanded. Good giving requires more than the donation of a check; it requires giving your heart.

Heartfelt giving, however, doesn't have to be foolish or naïve. Adopting an approach to philanthropy that combines an open heart with a sharp mind can be enriching for all. As we lean toward the actual work we support, we recognize there are few easy solutions. Instead, what emerges is a humble commitment towards long-term investment, involvement, and transformation.

Many wealthy entrepreneurs approach philanthropy the way they've approached their business careers: as a problem to fix. And why not? Little has stood in their way that couldn't be fixed with some elbow grease. But giving well is not about just-in-time delivery and larger-scale production lines. People are not widgets. Changing culture, social systems, and the habits and hearts of people—the work of charity—is a multi-faceted challenge: it is slow, incremental, and painfully complicated, involving the contribution of human capital as well as financial capital.

Embracing a generous lifestyle begins to break down us-versus-them barriers that divide the haves from the have-nots. Slowly we recognize we need one another.

This type of engagement is not new, but it does contrast with the stereotype of philanthropy that is typically seen and applauded in our society. In the prevailing model, tuxedos and cocktail dresses are more common than blue jeans; large plaques laud the donor; and giving satisfies the vacuum in the donor's soul rather than joining it together with others in a common cause. Traditional giving tosses a few coins in a discarded coffee cup or guitar case, then walks off without a second thought about the systems that lead to an individual to warm himself on a subway grate on a sub-zero February night.

A concept that has guided me is that a philanthropic life is one of pilgrimage, a journey of change and evolution towards life in a new world.

Beginnings

It requires us to cultivate the willingness to let go, to surrender. Not only is money released on this journey, but we also adopt a new, freer attitude. It can be a humbling experience to surrender with open hands. We learn through mistakes, failures, and successes as we walk down the road. Hopefully one day the sun breaks through to warm our backs.

Traditional philanthropy shows up for the photo-op with an oversized check, but a commitment to deeper philanthropy stays long after the reporters have left the scene. Philanthropists ready to go on pilgrimage will contribute more than money, will patiently wait for long-term impact, and will discover surprising, humbling change in themselves as they walk forward.

Such philanthropists take an approach of stewardship, believing we are given something "in trust" for someone else, and that we must give an account of our handling of that resource. We view our philanthropy as a process of managing something that does not truly belong to us. We are entrusted with the task of seeing fruitfulness come from the resource.

Pilgrimages have a beginning, a middle, and an end. In philanthropy, I'm only in the middle of the journey—I haven't yet arrived at my destination, and in fact, to be honest, sometimes I'm not always sure of my route. But, as people on pilgrimage do, I'm learning and growing as I walk along the way of managing resources for charitable impact.

Conversations for your pilgrimage

1. How have you defined your philanthropy?
2. Are you ready to be changed by your philanthropy?

2

A countercultural journey

San Sebastián (Day 1)

At dawn, I gathered with twenty pilgrims in the kitchen where we took turns sitting in the twelve available seats. It was a bleary-eyed group. No one talked, no relationships had yet been formed—we were careful to preserve proper boundaries on this first morning. To be truthful, most of us didn't even know what language the person next to us was thinking in. But as we buttered our bread and sipped our coffees, conversations tentatively sprouted in French, Spanish, German and, lastly, English.

I launched out by 6:30 and walked alone through the urban fringes of this border town, following yellow arrows painted on the road, signposts, rocks, and buildings. The sky was cloudy, and it was cool—a good day to walk as long as the rain held off. Cement soon gave way to marshland and forest, then an ascent to the Ermita de Guadalupe, a religious shrine at the top of the crest. After a few hours of solitary walking, I fell into step with a younger couple, and we quickly introduced ourselves: Adam and Maria Ann were young Hungarians from Budapest, he an actor and she a nanny.

As we walked, we made small talk. I mentioned wanting to write this book, and Adam, searching for the right English words, said that I needed the kiss of someone whose name he could only recall in Hungarian. I finally realized he was referring to the muses—those legendary Greek women who would honor someone with the gift of inspiration. I agreed; yes, I did need that kiss.

We later separated, and after strenuous coastal mountains, I eventually arrived in San Sebastián, a beach city graced with the density that urban

9

planners love—all residential buildings seven stories tall with the ground floor as retail. Today's walk had been twenty-six kilometers and I had pushed myself to my limit; I literally had no energy left. Rather than spending more time searching for the official albergue, *I discovered a small pension where retired resident Elvira took me into one of her two rooms in an exceptionally beautiful and historic city center.*

Glorified in our society and envied by the other ninety-nine percent, the extremely wealthy seem to have it made. Advertising reinforces this attitude—celebrating the accumulation of the right possessions and enriching experiences for self and family. But behind the Rolex watches, spa vacations, and monster homes, are people really happier? Are they really more satisfied? Knowing the stories of many who live these lives makes me suspect not.

Life for the wealthy often extends very little beyond one's tight circle. In that way, the lifestyles of the rich and famous can be curiously impoverished, and, sadly, profoundly self-centered.

The majority of us don't live in the realm of the super rich but our hearts are infected with the virus of our culture's insistent demand to orient our lives materialistically. Our comfortable lives divorce us from an awareness of our deepest human need: to live lives of service, oriented toward giving to others and contributing to an enriched shared culture. When we live in isolation from real community, our "success" can turn into alienation, depression, disintegrating relationships, and addictions.

Nowhere were these miserable qualities more evident than in the peculiar First World problem of hoarding. The Australian organization guru, Peter Walsh, helps people declutter their lives. Walsh guides families through the process of divorcing themselves from drowning in their stuff. In extreme cases, homes, offices, garages, and storage units are filled to the rafters with excess cargo—useless consumer items that sit unused and often in their original packaging.

Sadder still than hoarding is the legacy of living life in orientation to things rather than people. These choices don't make people happier or more productive. Hoarders don't become more engaged in community life. Instead, they become paralyzed by their possessions. In his book, *It's All Too Much: An Easy Plan for Living a Richer Life with Less Stuff*, Walsh challenges readers to answer a very simple but perhaps threatening question: "Does the stuff you own contribute to the life you hope to live, or is it really a hurdle that is getting in the way of your happiness?"[1]

Research by Michael Norton, assistant professor at Harvard Business School, and Elizabeth Dunn, assistant psychology professor at the University of British Columbia, confirms that money doesn't buy happiness. In an interview in *Canadian Business* they state: "Taking your bonus pay and showering yourself with gifts won't make you happy, but being generous will. Even among the most selfish employees, it was only the amount they spent on others that led to increased happiness."[2]

These researchers confirm a truth: the best antidote to consumerism is giving generously to others. But how do those of us who have been conditioned to seek happiness by purchasing more inventory learn instead to surrender the stuff and love giving well?

Living and working with poor communities for several years in developing nations such as Colombia and the Philippines radically reoriented my understanding of wealth and poverty. The people we worked with had little in the way of material goods, and their lack often shocked us. However, over time our friends proved to us that they were wealthy in many other ways: in creativity, perseverance, laughter, and a high value for relationships.

One day in the coffee-growing mecca of Manizales, Colombia, Karen and I were invited to a couple's home for dinner. Javier and Carmen were local pastors of the Cruzada Cristiana church, and had become colleagues in our work of resourcing and equipping local church leaders. Their lives had recently taken a tragic turn when they discovered their toddler was completely deaf, and would therefore face a life of dependence and need. We saw each other several times a week, and they were frequent visitors in our home. We were pleased to be able to be their guests and this was the first time we had been invited into their home.

---

1 Walsh, *It's All Too Much*, 52.
2 Prashad, "Compensation," para. 1.

Beginnings

Karen and I climbed the rickety exterior set of stairs of a tenement, and paused at the doorway of an apartment that was barely furnished with a few meager items. Javier beckoned us in with a grin. We socialized while Carmen finished off preparing the meal, and when it was ready, they motioned for us to sit. Before us were two chairs, two plates, two spoons, and two glasses. Confused and embarrassed, we asked if they were going to join us. Matter-of-factly and with humor, they replied that that was all they had—we were going to take turns. So we ate, they washed up the plates, and then they ate. We told jokes, we laughed, and we shared stories of raising our kids. Friendship was strengthened as they trusted us enough to bring us into their home. Though it lacked some of the amenities of ours, they didn't let that stop them from generously opening their doors to us. They knew our friendship wouldn't suffer when they revealed the extent of their physical poverty.

What impressed me with this interaction was our friends' lack of shame despite not having what we perceived as the essential tools for hospitality. We felt privileged that they felt close enough to us to not let that be a barrier. From this couple we learned that hospitality is about attitude and not about the trappings. Javier and Carmen honored us through an open-hearted generosity, giving out of the few possessions they had, but also sharing with us the wealth of a trusting relationship. This simple couple lived philanthropically.

I remember this generous friendship whenever I reflect on the poverty of our culture. There are heavy, mind-numbing responsibilities that come with stewarding one's successes: managing a complicated financial portfolio, homes, a cottage, boats and vehicles, not to mention multiple business units and the needs of employees. Our homes are filled with items to enable hospitality. But I've been in columned mansions and feasted at elaborate buffets where I felt less generosity than I experienced in the simple apartment of Javier and Carmen.

We are faced with a choice. We can remain self-absorbed and sedated by the allure of comfort and end up curiously impoverished. Or, we can emerge from our protective shells and engage with our world. This is the opportunity offered through a humble approach to philanthropy. A wealth of experiences, relationships, and giving awaits us.

In my journey of stewardship, I have learned that all people are potential philanthropists as we all have something to share with one another. This call to philanthropy means living outside our narrow, self-focused world.

We all must steward whatever is in our hands, and generously live life for others.

Conversations for your pilgrimage

1. What is in your hands?

2. Can you give freely and generously from whatever you find there?

3

Motivations behind giving

Orio (Day 2)

I awoke and peered out the window at the San Sebastián streets that had been filled with inebriated tourists only a few hours earlier. The empty pavement below glistened with moisture from a soft rain. I breathed in and steeled myself: I was going to get wet on my second day of walking. After eggs, a scrap of dry baguette, and coffee, I dug my poncho from the deepest recesses of my backpack and draped it over my frame. I knew that if Karen could see me with my backpack hidden underneath my poncho, she would call me the hunchback of Notre Dame.

Like yesterday, and like many more days to come along the Camino del Norte, the trail would take me up and over a mountain ridge then down into the next harbor on the path. I had an app on my phone that helpfully provided elevation maps and distances, and a printed guidebook in my pack that was turning out to be not much good at all due to its vagueness. But mainly, one navigates the camino *merely by following the painted yellow arrows that sprout up on lamp posts, the back of road signs, curbs, rocks, and sides of buildings. It was like a giant game of I Spy. Sometimes if I wasn't vigilant, I might miss an arrow, and would dead end in an alley, or after fifteen minutes of not seeing arrows, it would gradually dawn on me that I had to backtrack to regain my trail.*

After yesterday's exertions I was hurting. I barely stopped to gaze at the spectacular views of cliffs and surf. When I arrived in the small town of Orio, I passed by a tranquil rural house that served as the albergue, *the occasional pilgrim shelters that routinely appear along the* camino. *I decided to call it a day. Twelve kilometers was enough today. Be kind to yourself, I could hear Karen saying.*

This practice became a typical routine: walk from dawn to early afternoon, then arrive at the albergue. *Gratefully shower, change clothes, attend to laundry. Then meander down to the town square for lunch. Adopting the practices of the locals, my lunch became my main meal, and I ate on their clock, around two or three in the afternoon. Then I would head back to the* albergue *for a siesta—my feet would be inflamed and sore from exertion.*

I had arranged with Jaffer, an Indo-American pilgrim from Oregon by way of South Asia, to have dinner together this evening. I offered to make the meal in the shared albergue *kitchen. While in town, I found a grocery store and brought back fresh salmon filets, tomatoes, salad, bread, and wine. During our meal I learned he didn't eat meat, so I was glad I had by chance bought the fish. We had a fascinating, meaningful conversation and connected at once as we overlooked green mountains in the distance.*

My gift of dinner for my new friend was sincere, but also laden with ulterior motives: eating alone is not appealing. Likewise, philanthropists are highly esteemed for their apparent self-sacrificial commitment to society. People see donations with many zeroes as a sign of selflessness. As these amounts are so far removed from the actual capacity of most people, we make a jump in logic, uncritically lauding such breathtaking gifts.

But what is actually behind these flashy pledges? Is a donation to any charity—because it is large—always the right investment? Can such generous gifts also be imprudent, naïve, or even selfish?

The material benefit is obvious, and hopefully the donor has done her homework by giving strategically and in a way that truly benefits the charitable organization. But the Gospels remind us that it is not the amount that is given which is considered laudable—rather it is about the attitude of the donor's heart. The impoverished woman who gave her two cents to the temple treasury gave all that she had out of her poverty, and her offering was esteemed as being of more value than that of large donations given by the Pharisee sect. The Pharisees gave significant amounts with great aplomb and fanfare, but out of hearts that were jaded, bitter, and self-seeking.

What's behind a major donation varies widely. As my fundraiser friends meet the people on their hit list, they've often been stymied: there's no single approach that seems to work because the people they meet don't fit their preconceived ideas of the wealthy. There are larger-than-life personalities and quiet church mice; those who give liberally, even rashly, and those who ask painstakingly detailed questions or construct unrealistic barriers to effective charity operations. Unfortunately, there are also those who throw their weight around, with demands and unrealistic requirements for the charity using their money. For these sorts, money is power, and it is abused in its deployment.

So what underlying motives might move a philanthropist? Motivations are as varied as the givers. Consider these various reasons for giving:

1. *"Giving to get"*: I walked into my office one morning and discovered a large cardboard box sitting on my desk. Deliveries like this aren't that unusual—often it is the gift of a book, or perhaps a small handmade artifact from a developing country, sent to me as a way to bridge the donor with work done through sponsored projects. But this box was big. And the sender was not an organization we had previously sponsored, but rather one I knew had their sights set on us as a potential funder of their African community transformation project.

   Ripping open the packaging, I held in my hands a rather heavy, elongated, bubble-wrapped item. As the folds fell away, I realized it was not an African wood carving as I had imagined, but an expensive $50 bottle of wine from an up-and-coming Okanagan, BC winery. Perplexed, I dug through the foam peanuts for an explanation. I found it in a long, gilded envelope containing an embossed invitation asking my wife and me to a spectacular and intimate evening featuring an exclusive performance by some award-winning artists.

   I started to tally the costs for us to attend this Vancouver fundraiser: round-trip airline tickets, car rental and lodging in the city, the $1,000 per person cost to attend. And then I added up the costs to the organization: the cost of the gift of unrequested wine, courier costs, printing costs, a five-star chef, a five-course meal with more wines, an honorarium to the performers.

Certain costs were likely donated as gifts-in-kind from suppliers—although there was no way of knowing. But the impression given was of exclusivity and luxury.

Nowhere did the invitation speak of the need in the African community. Nowhere did they seek our engagement in the lives of people on the ground. Nowhere did they even announce that there would be an opportunity to invest in the ongoing development of this organization's mission.

This attempt distressed me as it seemed out of sync with what I hoped were the good intentions of the organization. Their approach was a common strategy seen in fundraising circles: that you have to woo potential donors to your mission by appealing to their own selfish interests. A fancy meal, a private concert—the idea that you get something back for your generosity. But that doesn't resonate with me as good philanthropy.

I feel the same way about certain hospital or charity lotteries: enter to win a chance at a million-dollar dream home, with one in four being a winner. Yes, there is a transfer of wealth to charities, but this is not philanthropy either. Behind these examples is a motivation of giving is to get, not primarily to invest in changed lives, or to even be changed oneself. It authenticates and validates our own selfish behaviors, and numbs the donor from truly engaging with the world outside their own.

2. *"Giving to make myself feel better"*: What could be more compelling than giving generously when news of the tsunami which devastated Indian Ocean communities? Seeing a quarter million people perish, entire towns washed out to sea, and economies in shambles prompted an unusual outpouring of support. Social agencies and governments hurriedly collaborated to respond to the unprecedented $7 billion in donations for aid. In the face of such a calamity, our own grantmaking committee chose to waive our established process, and sent an immediate gift to a trusted partner who had feet on the ground in these communities. It seemed inhumane not to respond with some sort of immediate donation of cash. But in retrospect, I often wonder whether we took the right course of action.

In the flurry of activity and funds transfers that occurred in the weeks after the disaster, we heard very little back from our partner on the effectiveness of this donation. We felt disconnected from what was accomplished through our gift.

If you want to give strategically, it is legitimate to doubt the effectiveness of sending large amounts of funds to emergency situations when the money arrives long after the crisis has passed. In the fog of disaster, money flows like water and inevitably decisions are made far from the grassroots, resulting in ineffectual and inappropriate solutions for the affected populace.

Holden Karnofsky, the Harvard-educated author of the Give Well blog, which advocates for smarter giving, reflects on this reality in his post, "The case against disaster relief":

> When a natural disaster and humanitarian crisis hits the headlines, many of us (including me) reach straight for our wallets. Emergencies have an easier time getting our attention (and emotional investment) than the chronic health problems that plague the developing world every day. But [. . .] emergency aid is one of the worst uses of donations, despite being one of the most emotionally compelling.[1]

Giving in emergency situations can show how our giving is often more about us than it is those we are trying to help. We feel better when we give to emergencies, but if it isn't all that effective, why do it? Instead, the majority of our giving needs to selectively invest in solutions that offer a more reasoned, long-term approach for these same communities.

3. *"I want to give back"*: The language of "giving back" is frequently used to describe philanthropic action. But what are the underlying assumptions loaded into this phrase? If a philanthropist gives to "give back" to society, what has been "taken" or "robbed" from them in the first place? The language seems to infer a measure of guilt behind the motivation of giving.

Some people may legitimately feel guilt for being wealthy, assuming that the ethics behind the earning of the wealth were not entirely above board. If business practices were built on the unethical treatment of employees, degrading the environment, or questionable

---

1. Karnofsky, "Disaster Relief," lines 1–6.

financial transactions, perhaps the need to give back does serve a purpose. However, a better way forward would be to develop an ethical framework that is consistent for both one's business dealings and philanthropic pursuits, and to strive to live an integrated life.

4. *"I want to help the poor"*: This altruistic desire to benefit those less economically fortunate is another motivation. It divides people into the haves and have-nots, and assumes a materialistic understanding of life. It positions the giver as one who has, and the receiver as one who needs.

    The problem with this approach is sometimes that it is based on the assumption that the materially poor have nothing to offer. It defines them based on material need alone, objectifying them, rather than viewing them as part of the human family who are able to offer much in relationship. As well, it also assumes that the wealthy have no needs, and are only in the position of givers, not receivers.

    Like the example of Carmen and Javier, those who receive our funds are actually very wealthy in many ways we are not. We have much to receive from them, if only we will open our hands, not only to give but to receive. When we recognize and receive the wealth they have to share with us, we grant them dignity.

    My friends, Chris and Phileena Heuertz, founders of Gravity, a center for contemplative activism in Omaha, Nebraska, have invested their lives in creating communities of love and service in the most demanding *barrios*, red light districts, and refugee camps of the urban developing world. They often speak of the commodification of the poor—treating them on the basis of their income level, rather than as people with hearts, passions, relationships, creativity, and intelligence—and something to offer the world. Philanthropists can and will give, but an even greater challenge is to learn to receive from those with whom they partner.

5. *"I want to be known"*: Few will admit to the motivation of giving because we want to be known and admired for our giving, but if we are completely honest, this motivation does exist. It may be exhilarating to see one's name on a hospital wing or university building. Being known for generosity is a way to advance your brand within the community, and can be a form of marketing.

Buying access and credibility in a community is a sad commentary on our society; perhaps we can view it as the commoditization of the wealthy as social standing becomes a purchased good.

6. *"I want to invest in my community"*: A better motivation might be to invest where one has put down roots. This means giving out of a sense of gratitude to a community—for being the place we have enjoyed a stable life, established a successful career, launched our children to independence, and been in relationship with loyal employees who live nearby. Investing in our community allows philanthropy to remain close to the action and rooted in the soil of relationships. Awareness of local conditions and needs are more acute, and we can see the results of our investment. During my tenure at Bridgeway Foundation, we determined to invest 10 percent of our total annual disbursement budget into our local community. This allowed our philanthropy to have a footprint on the ground, and positioned us as contributors into the local nonprofit conversation.

7. *"I want to reform charity"*: Entrepreneurs can tackle anything with passion and creativity in the movement known as social entrepreneurship. Indeed, the charitable sector has much to learn from the marketplace; we are impoverished if we neglect business principles in our nonprofit work.

    My own story is one of working within the nonprofit sector for a decade before launching out in running our family foundation. I admit that the ten years of experiencing the weaknesses of organizational life as a charity employee led me to emphasize funding in order to strengthen the capacity of charities. Building the capacity of charities to be run more professionally, to treat their employees with dignified human resources practices, and to operate with reasonable tools to raise the bar on their outputs are reforms that are frequently needed.

8. *"I want to express gratitude"*: Gratitude as a motive behind giving recognizes that the ability to create wealth is not solely located in the entrepreneur, but in a host of other variables: economic conditions, a society based on free market principles, the commitment and skill of coworkers, even place of birth or the ability to immigrate to a nation where economic growth is possible.

The object of our gratitude may be society in general, or if religiously motivated, one's Creator. The biblical injunction that "everyone who has been given much, much is required" speaks of the need to utilize our resources for the benefit of others. Saying thanks in a tangible way with our money is a motivation for many donors.

9. *"To fulfill one's purpose in being human"*: This motivation recognizes that we are not made to hoard, but to give. Giving is fulfilling part of our DNA—it is an aspect of being fully human. We are made to be in relationship, not isolated, and giving allows us the opportunity to become more woven into the fabric of our community.

   Perhaps this is one of the reasons behind one of Jesus' enigmatic statements that we would always have the poor among us. The poor need the wealthy—but the wealthy also need the poor. And we need to have the poor among us, living in diversified communities and networks of relationship. This reality forces us out of self-centered living, out of our tendency to migrate towards an insulated bubble where we exist with others just like us. If we acquire or possess wealth, it is a resource to be used to serve broader society with generosity, grace, and self-sacrifice. It is an opportunity for us to be engaged with society and become part of the solution.

Motivations behind giving are complex, and are frequently a mix of many of these reasons cited. None of us have untainted motives. When we give gifts, we seem to do so with a measure of selflessness, stirred together with a little ego; we attach some strings and an agenda or two, and top it off with a note of gratitude.

Conversations for your pilgrimage

1. What mix of motivations currently guide your philanthropy?

2. Are there any you would you add to your mix? Which would you prefer to let go?

Structure and process

Se hace camino al andar.
You make the way by walking.
–Antonio Machado[2]

---

2. Machado, "Proverbios XXIX," line 4. Translated by author.

4

Starting with good intentions

Zumaia (Day 3)

My ears opened before my eyes. The middle-aged Austrian couple in the bunk bed next to mine apparently didn't know how to whisper, and they wore annoying portable headlamps that shone light into my face as they repacked their bags. Their gruff voices echoed through the albergue *where twenty-five of us were still trying to sleep.*

Since gray pre-morning light was already announcing a new day, I resigned myself to getting up. I splashed cold water on my face, brushed my teeth, took a swig of water, and set out by 6:30.

My feet and hips ached as I walked down a steep hill into the town center and across the bridge over the river which emptied into the sea. But soon I gained my rhythm: up and down another ridge and an hour and a half later I found myself in the seaside town of Zarautz. By this time the cafés were opening, workers were setting out aluminum chairs and tables, and umbrellas began sprouting like dandelions. I savored my first coffee of the day along with an irresistible palmera, *a tightly woven pastry in the shape of a palm tree coated with dark chocolate. But I was happy to leave the beach scene with its wakening tourists—it felt fake and contrived.*

The path hugged rugged cliffs and followed the main road between towns along the coast. At this point the camino took the shape of an ocean-front promenade, traffic whizzing by on one side, surf pounding on the other. After Getaria it wound inland—uphill again, of course, offering magnificent views of cliffs and seascapes, and finally winding down once again at the town of Zumaia.

The main albergue in Zumaia was the cavernous convent of San Martin. I arrived just as it opened for new pilgrim arrivals, and waited in the common room with two French couples who had preceded me. Many Europeans, like these folks, walk the camino during their summer holidays—taking one or two weeks to walk various stages, and returning in subsequent years to continue. A nun showed me to my room—a glorious semi-private with a real bed on the floor and no creaky bunk beds around. The austerity and tranquility was all I wanted and needed. She also indicated that mass was held at seven in the evening, and that I was welcome.

The bells started ringing fifteen minutes prior and the church was magnificent. Romanesque, and dating from the twelfth century, it spoke of longevity and permanence. How many generations had lived and died while this church stood witness to faith, even during the darkest days of Moorish occupation or Franco's dictatorship? I arrived, expecting to understand the Spanish mass, but was jolted by the confusing Euskara tongue—I was, after all, in Basque Country. Like the Québécois in Canada, the Basques are a nation within a nation, and they are proud of their identity and unique language. Just about any Euskara word would score over fifty in Scrabble as the words are jam-packed with Xs, Ks, Zs, and Js. It is unrecognizable to any other language I know. The priest and readers alternated randomly between Euskara and Spanish, so at least I understood half of the mass.

The first reading focused on the story of Joseph in Egypt, when his brothers came years after their betrayal in search of food for the family. Joseph's hopeful and faith-filled perspective—that God has a redemptive purpose despite years of incomprehensible events—was moving. As we considered the complexity and breadth of our lives, I remembered again that all can be redeemed.

Leaving the church and drawn to the town center, I happened to run into Jaffer, my companion from the previous evening. He was with Hazif, a Moroccan-Belgian. They asked me to join them for dinner. We had an enjoyable evening comparing stories. No matter the background, no matter the faith, the camino brings people together on a journey. You must be open, not closed; receptive, not judgmental. Where else could I spend time with progressive Muslims who themselves are on a journey of faith and openness to God's love?

In the late nineties when my parents were suddenly faced with a large endowment for the foundation that had, for years, just been an idea, we had no experience with large-scale philanthropy. The transaction occurred in an instant, but it took us years to sort out the ramifications of such a decision and to move ahead with confidence in our work. In the beginning all we had were good intentions to guide us in our work. And indeed, we believed at the time that it would be an easy thing to give away money for worthy charitable work.

We were five siblings spread apart over a twenty-year stretch, raised by two generous, committed parents. Well before the foundation was endowed, our parents had raised us with principles that oriented us towards living generously and with a view to service within our community. Any charitable donation was always done quietly by my parents, with little or no visibility in the community or even within our family. They modeled to us that great philanthropy starts with repeated, small acts done with open hearts. Years later I would learn of their generous and thoughtful interventions to assist vulnerable individuals or families—not just through the donation of funds, but through Dad offering his wisdom through financial counselling or Mom offering her friendship and serving meals with a personal and gracious touch. They practiced a lifestyle of philanthropy long before I ever heard the term.

It was with this sort of sincere generosity motivated by their Christian faith that they began operating their suddenly endowed foundation. Within their networks were many service-oriented individuals who worked in the charitable sector, and through these friendships they began giving to their friends' charities.

Foundations face regulations regarding their endowments: in Canada, one must disburse 3.5 percent of the market value of the foundation from the previous two-year period's average. "Qualified donees" (i.e., charities) must be the beneficiaries. Faced with this requirement, my parents found themselves under annual pressure in the week after Christmas to disburse funds before the end of the calendar year.

Handwritten notes by my mother accompanied large checks to these organizations. Undoubtedly, the amounts that were given would have been among the charity's largest gifts in the year. During these initial years, year-end giving was done with a general awareness of the goodness of the organization's work, based on a friendly relationship with the charity's personnel, and nothing but a friendly acknowledgement response was ever expected.

Many generous Christians take seriously the biblical exhortation "not to let your left hand know what the right hand is doing" as the motivation for being discreet and anonymous in their philanthropy. By necessity, this metaphor breaks down when your giving is done through a foundation that publicly reports its annual donations to government authorities and where information about all donations is available to anyone with a web browser. The decision to set up a foundation suddenly breaks down one's ability to remain anonymous. For foundations, greater transparency and clarity become the norm as one is no longer acting as a private individual.

There's nothing wrong with giving with just good intentions when personal donations are small; such honest motivations guide much charitable giving today. However, with larger donations at play, good intentions reveal themselves to be an approach that is lacking on various levels. Time and again this method was shown to be ineffectual, and proved, in fact, to be a poor approach to stewarding wisely the assets of our foundation. We had started off on the journey with sincerity of heart, but needed to mature.

First was the challenge with giving larger amounts. A charity that effectively handled a small, unrestricted $1,000 gift, was not necessarily capable of absorbing and adequately utilizing a $50,000 donation. With smaller donations, a donor trusts that the funds will be used for a much larger project where their gift is only one of many that make up the project value. But with increased donation size, one significant check can essentially underwrite an entire project or an annual salary. The responsibility tied to this act of generosity then no longer exclusively belongs to the charity; responsibility needs to be shared with the giver to ensure the investment being made is one that adds constructive value to the organization's outreach and is in line with the priorities of the giver.

In our foundation's early years in the late 1990s, we witnessed many cases where our donated funds languished at nominal interest rates in the charity's bank account for months or even years. We gave funds without the charity having a plan to effectively deploy them. These funds could have been more profitably invested if we had retained the cash. Sadly, there were also cases where the unexpected lottery-like arrival of funds was rashly applied to activity later seen to be ineffective or out of sync with the giver's priorities or the organization's capacity to effectively deliver on their promises.

Another perplexing issue was relational. Donations were frequently given based on existing personal friendships with charity personnel. Our granting was a function of these relationships. With no application process, getting the ear of a family member seemed to be the best approach to pave the way for a successful grant. Unfortunately, this allowed a dysfunctional pattern to emerge where lack of clarity, strings-attached relationships, and unspoken expectations were the norm. The parameters of the original friendships were suddenly changed with the significant bankrolling of a charity's activities. This eventually led to misunderstandings and a sense of unease from both parties because of the changing dynamics and lack of clarity about the relationships.

Because there were fuzzy parameters surrounding the donations in these early years, and due to our patterns in giving, another situation began to evolve: that of an ongoing expectation of an annual donation in December. Charity budgets began to be formulated based on this expectation. This puts the donor in a challenging position. If an employee's salary could be financed through one unrestricted annual donation, a donor's veering from this pattern could have serious and unintended consequences. Because our early giving was done without communicating expectations on both sides of the table, a looming problem began to arise.

When a donor's giving ranks in the top ten of a charity's income streams, significant care must be taken to give wisely with a rationale for how your investment will be used. It is an investment that will impact the livelihood of individuals, and will determine the charity's action plan for the next period of time. With our early giving, we failed to realize that when we rescued an organization with large donations, we did not allow them the opportunity to build competencies in creating a broader donor base. It is far healthier for charities to rely on a solid, diffused base of support rather than a single large donor, allowing for greater long-term sustainability. It is also healthier for the donor, who then has the freedom to explore other meaningful initiatives.

We came to see that our "good intentions" approach and naiveté in granting also had the unfortunate effect of insulating the organization from dealing with realities that are exposed when a charity's funds are tight. When large grants arrive on the doorstep of an organization, things like the lack of strong leadership, a deficient strategy, or internal conflict are often covered over with the veneer of success. In those days, our grants were often in the top five grants an organization might receive. Our annual donation implied our ongoing endorsement of the organization, and we had a responsibility to think through our granting in a more professional manner.

The endowment of the foundation brought another unexpected issue to the table. Suddenly our foundation began cropping up on lists of other endowed foundations, and mail and phone calls began arriving at my parents' home address. A year's worth of proposals would be piled several feet high. The time and money that charities invested into these elaborate, unrequested proposals was substantial, and it was a shame that most of it went unread into the recycling bin. As well, people began requesting meetings with the principals of our foundation. The vast majority of these inquiries were of no interest to our family, but time had to be expended to manage the volume, attend to the calls, and a strategic direction needed to be decided upon and communicated. Failing to do this would waste everyone's time and money—charities and foundation alike.

Before long, we recognized that our giving through the foundation brought more stress and less joy than we had hoped. The reason behind this was simply that we lacked a clear strategy and had failed to communicate it. By adopting a defined philanthropic agenda, communication plan, and capable personnel, stresses could be minimized and the joy could return. My parents set up their foundation with the view that giving to others was a natural part of being contributing members of a community, never expecting there would be significant issues around managing an endowment and complying with the annual mandate to effectively disburse grants.

The decision to formalize operations into a more strategic management of our philanthropy allowed us to overcome these earlier challenges. At the end of 2000, I was hired as the first executive director in order to apply time and energy towards leading the foundation. My first items of business were to develop our strategic direction, receive the endorsement of family members, and establish internal systems to facilitate smooth functioning for communication flow, grant request consideration, and approved grant monitoring. It was evident to me that we would also need to develop a website to communicate our priorities to the wider public.

Getting strategic priorities right and communicating them well is important. Many foundations struggle with this question, and end up selecting an area of interest to focus on. This may be thematic—such as kids at risk, human trafficking, the arts, international development, or education; or perhaps geographic, with roots in a local community and the desire to contribute to the social fabric of life in one's city, province, state, or country. These decisions are informed by the experience of the founders. One man I admire struggled with and held off kidney cancer for four years through an organic diet and natural remedies, and during this period created a foundation to fund research for this disease in the future. In our case, our family's Christian faith played a significant role in the creation and disbursement of the endowment, so this became the underlying thread that wove through our grantmaking.

Our attempt to define our philanthropic purpose involved a period of assessment and strategic planning, something we didn't rush. I recommend the approach to givers both large and small. Know your mission, and follow a written plan for your philanthropy. Be able to define why you are giving. The parameters of your giving program will allow you to say no with confidence and without embarrassment, and to say yes with enthusiasm. Thinking through principles around your giving before the heat of the charity's enthusiastic pitch will be ultimately empowering to you.

In our case, we selected outsiders to lead us through this process. It felt risky to invite someone from outside our family to help us because until then, we had always considered our philanthropy to be a private and personal matter. However, too much was at stake, so we invited trusted advocates who offer strategic planning services to help us define our purpose and goals. It is a very vulnerable thing to open your family and giving to other perspectives, but it was a healthy process to open up communication within our own family, and put our goals and objectives in writing so we could all sing from the same hymnbook, so to speak.

Giving by family foundations is typically an intensely private matter with a small group of related people involved in the decision-making. However, new foundations should not be shy about seeking assistance from others who can offer wisdom and perspective. Family dynamics are established early and each person is an expert at playing their given role—"father," "mother," "eldest sibling," "middle child," and "baby of the family"—having spent their entire lives learning these roles. A new foundation is not the place to continue playing these family roles if the goal is to become a reasonably healthy organization. Consultants who specialize in this area know the types of questions to ask, and can offer an approach for a family to define a giving strategy that will allow all members an opportunity to share ownership in the strategic direction. Inviting trusted confidantes into the development of the foundation's mission will be empowering for the family.

Conversations for your pilgrimage

1. Has your family discussed what your philanthropic priorities are?
2. Have you developed a written strategic plan for your philanthropy? If not, who would be a good resource person to assist you?

5

Setting priorities

Today Jaffer and I decided to walk together, and for the first time, I would have a companion while walking. On my first day of walking, when I happened to fall in step with him on the path between Irún and San Sebastián, he was in such pain and moving so slowly that he had begged me to not slow down but to go on ahead. Today, however, he was in better form so while I set the pace, he kept up.

Jaffer is a retired systems engineer from Oregon, seventy years young, a PhD, and he loves to tell stories. I'm a good listener so it was enjoyable interacting with him about issues such as complexity theory. With our western minds, we interpret life as cause-and-effect, and think that if we can just manipulate the variables, we can make it better. But our society is crumbling from within, showing that our attempts at conquering and subduing the planet aren't sustainable. Embracing a theory of complexity allows for ambiguity, and I believe it's the only way to truly have faith. It's also a position of humility, recognizing that we are limited in our ability to influence the outcomes we desire.

I probed a bit into Jaffer's unusual faith story as he had alluded to being nominally Muslim but more recently has found space to believe by attending a Quaker meeting house. He said he loves to go into the room and sit in silence for an hour together with the community.

I admired his spiritual journey that takes risks and creates a space for ambiguity. Within my own spiritual culture, we seem to prioritize church shopping, flashy multimedia, and Bible answer men who seem to have all the answers. Many churches in Canada are more focused on congregants as consumers of products than on living by faith into the mysteries of grace, redemption, and resurrection. In time we will discover what is more sustainable and enduring.

Each of the days so far have seemed the same—climb for a few hours, descend for a few hours to the next harbor town. Now we descended into Deba, a town cloistered at the mouth of a river at the Cantabrian Sea. The descent was so steep that the slope thankfully had been turned into steps, and then, before us, lay a surprising feature: rather than more stairs, two consecutive public, outdoor elevators took us the remaining ten stories downward to the main streets of the town below. As we squeezed shoulder to shoulder into the confined space of the elevator with Basques going about their daily business, I was acutely embarrassed by our pilgrim stench from walking all day in the heat.

Our albergue *this evening was the former railroad station whose upper two floors were converted into a modern European hostel. There, I met up with Thierry and Manuela, a French couple from Lyon, Alain from La Rochelle, and Maria, a Bavarian woman who dragged me along to dinner. Maria didn't speak French or English, so conversation her way was translated into German by Manuela. My rusty French was adequate, but led to many hilarious moments over the evening as we shared stories, and I butchered another European language along with the meatballs.*

Both my parents were raised in the 1940s and 1950s by fathers who were pastors in the same small, fundamentalist denomination that was characterized by a list of do's and don'ts attempting to legislate external behaviors. As pastors' kids in small Canadian towns, their comportment was under scrutiny in their churches, and love became their escape hatch. Before they reached twenty, they married and quickly abandoned their denomination for a somewhat broader evangelical perspective.

Faith was important to my parents. The evangelical faith they eventually embraced was not the fundamentalist sort that ghettoized its followers from society, but one that encouraged its members to engage as participating contributors to the whole. As a result, the types of organizations they wanted to fund were ones with similar approaches.

The selection of faith-based charities that engaged with the broader community as partners was strategic, and indicative of the world we live in. If the events of 9/11 taught Western society anything, it was that we are now living in a post-secular world. The world's faiths have risen again—for better or worse—to take prominence in questions of social makeup and civic discourse. Faith which was compartmentalized by modernism into influencing Sundays but not Mondays is quickly dissipating.

Post-secularism recognizes that religion, spirituality, or faith is an essential element of human existence; it's impossible and disingenuous to divorce spirituality from our public lives. The choice is no longer between either religious or non-religious expression. It is, rather, what kind of spiritual expression do we each offer our society where the choices of all members of society can be respected?

A focus on faith-based charities led us to a dilemma because expressing faith through charitable work is done in hundreds of possible ways with hundreds of kinds of clients. Many foundations zero in on activity defined by a program theme: international development, a particular health concern, youth employment skills, or other specific areas. In such cases, it becomes easier to both define who you partner with as well as what you are attempting to achieve through your philanthropic work. You set goals and measure your success in relationship to the benefit provided to these groups.

In our case, the clients we served were not a specific target group receiving programming, but the organizations themselves that serve a multiplicity of needs and issues. We view our clientele as the organizations, not the end beneficiaries, and the common linkage was these partners' commitment to operate out of their faith perspective in service to the broader community. We selected partnerships with organizations that have a broad and healthy sense of Christian mission in the world, and that are doing so in ways that allow our faith to be seen as a positive contributing element benefiting our entire multicultural, multi-faith society.

As a result, our partners include a wide range of organizations—from think tanks to international development charities, from the arts to inner city organizations working with the homeless, from venerable educational institutions to young organizations run by twentysomethings. The belief that faith must lead one to holistically contribute to one's society is what unites these disparate groups. These partners take risks to serve at the margins of society, bringing the good, the beautiful, and the true to their communities.

Early on, we also made the strategic decision to partner only with organizations that had already developed a donor base larger than $250,000 in annual revenue. While we were strongly attracted to the entrepreneurial vision and drive behind funding charitable start-ups, funding such entities required a completely different set of competencies and processes, and with our limited staffing we couldn't manage this.

Once we determined that any larger-sized, faith-based charity would be our constituency, we then selected two major areas where we could influence change. One of these emphases was innovation. We would partner with organizations that were exploring ways to innovate in their programming, to extend it further, or to launch a new initiative. We felt that major donor dollars invested in the innovation would make it possible more quickly. (In my view, a charity's donor constituency surrounds and supports its tried-and-true program activities, so partnering with a foundation like ours helped us play a unique and valuable role for the charity to expand its outreach.) Over time as the innovation became an accepted and celebrated part of the charity's mission, our hope was that it would become sustainable through the charity's regular donor base.

The second major area of emphasis for our strategy was to partner with organizations that needed "capacity building." Funding was not directed toward a charity's program where most charity fundraising efforts are directed. Instead, capacity building means funds are designated towards the strengthening of the organization's health and professionalization. Our partnerships took the form of a variety of capacity-building efforts: from updating technology to hiring a fundraiser, from renovating office space to providing the opportunity for a sabbatical for an overworked executive director. None of these grants were the typical funding geared for program outcomes, but were investments to impact the health of the organization, ultimately building a better context in which the charity could deliver needed charitable services.

While it is important to have a broad strategy, we also maintained flexibility within our plan to allow for some smaller impact that would give each of our family members a sense of ownership and contribution to the broader work of the foundation. This included a focus on local initiatives— the development of a fund for specific local initiatives such as the United Way, food banks, and hospitals to allow our family to sponsor initiatives close to home without regard to a faith affiliation.

As well, each family member was annually given an opportunity to sponsor a small grant to any Canadian Christian charity of their choice. Our only requirement was that the family member had to be actively volunteering or offering support in some way to the charity, and then the foundation would honor their volunteer support with a financial donation. This decision was an excellent way to enable family members to feel a part of the ongoing work of the foundation, as well as to cultivate our family's volunteer spirit of engagement in the non-profit sector.

Conversations for your pilgrimage

1. How would you articulate a strategy for your philanthropy?
2. Why have you developed this approach?

6

The need for a clear strategy

Markina-Xemein (Day 5)

Alain grabbed my foot this morning at 5:45 to waken me. Alain, Maria, Jaffer, and I had determined to leave early as we feared that the next town would not have sufficient hostel beds. As it was an isolated town, and our trek there today would be long and painful, we needed to set off early.

It was still black as we headed out, the lights of the town reflecting in the river as we crossed over the bridge. And then up, up, up. Over the next hour we suffered up a grueling 500-meter climb to the appropriately named Calvario as the early morning lightened the sky. Though it threatened rain all day, we were blessed with overcast skies and cooler temperatures as our trail led us into the mountains and away from the coastline.

At one crossroads in the predawn, Alain insisted the way went forward, but our maps showed we should turn left. He grumpily set off on his own, picking up two other pilgrims who took his side. Maria, Jaffer, and I moved along the left-hand branch. We knew the trails would merge again, but the other way was steeper and added distance to the hike.

We had been advised that there was only one café along our route today, five kilometers after we had ascended. It was just opening for coffee and toast as we walked by, so we were grateful to stop a moment. Other than that pause, we walked all day away from civilization into mature pine forests along a high mountain ridge. We were truly alone, encountering only a handful of people. It was a dramatic and beautiful walk.

The one thing I was missing was a staff. I had used a wooden staff on last year's camino, purchasing it with Nate in St-Jean before we began our hike, and becoming emotionally attached to this sturdy support. On the way home, the airline had refused to allow it in the cabin, so I had to check my pole. Somehow it didn't make it to my final destination, and I never was reunited with it.

Today was the first day I was beginning to regret not having the extra support. The climbs and descents were steep and the ground uneven. I mentioned this to Maria and Jaffer, who had technical walking poles, and they began to search along with me for a staff as we walked. All options they presented were too crooked, too short, too thin, or too heavy. I grew tired of having them dig in the bushes for options, and said, "Don't worry, my staff will come to me when it's time."

I know this is hard to believe, but within a few minutes of those words leaving my mouth, a Basque man suddenly emerged in the woods alongside us holding a handsaw. Without us saying a word, he boldly shouted to me through the forest, "Hey, you need a staff!"

The man turned back into the bush, found a holly tree, and sawed off the straight top section. He quickly rid the branch of the smaller twigs, and within minutes, presented me with a perfectly formed Basque staff. I inquired his name and he replied, Antonio. Humbled and astonished by the miraculous gift, I told him no, he was actually San Antonio del Bosque (Saint Anthony of the Forest). We laughed and he walked along with us for a bit, pointing out his log cabin hidden among the pines, and showing us where to find the chamomile flowers he had picked for tea.

The path downward to Markina-Xemein was intense and steep, but after eight challenging hours walking, we limped into this hardscrabble logging town. Maria miraculously still had energy and wanted to reach a monastery that took in pilgrims another seven kilometers away, but Jaffer and I were spent. We followed signs to a private albergue and then a late lunch, before crashing with exhaustion into our siesta.

Structure and process

Many donors long to develop a strategic approach to their philanthropy. They seek an issue, a cause, which inflames their giving. With their foundations, they identify an on-the-ground issue of importance so their money and involvement begins to chip away at the concerns of the world. This often springs from their own areas of competence or personal background, allowing them to offer a constructive approach.

These choices are strategic. Each of these donors identifies their own program area, and pursues solutions, declining involvement in other competing concerns. They often end up being advocates for influencing the development of systems, leading to involvement in political pressure and media campaigns for change. This approach to philanthropy is not so much concerned with grantmaking as it is "change-making."

Whether giving large or small amounts, giving becomes much more meaningful when you strategically invest in charities that reflect your passions. Rather than just climbing on the bandwagon of the latest trendy causes, research the most meaningful way to add value. Settling into a defined strategic purpose for your giving is an empowering tool that advances the grantmaker's interests, and frees you to say no to competing requests with grace.

Defining this purpose is essential because of a prominent misconception about philanthropy: people think that giving away money must be both fun and easy. A few years ago, Guerrilla Giving, based in Vancouver, developed a novel approach to philanthropy.[1] This anonymous family decided to give away 10 percent of their gross income through a simple methodology. Guerrilla Giving selects a random location each day—say in a mound of pumpkins at the farmers' market, or inside the pages of a free community newspaper given away at the supermarket—and they plant twenty dollars' cash along with a note instructing the finder to use it in any way they find appropriate. The assumption is that they will empower individuals to channel funds towards their own charitable acts, or perhaps that the finder has their own pertinent need the money can be used for. Occasionally the finder will report back in the comments of the Guerilla Giving blog as to what was achieved through the gift, but realistically, one assumes most of the funds are pocketed and used on expensive lattes.

While their approach is certainly generous and seems to be motivated by good intentions, I believe that it is bad philanthropy. It is neither strategic nor does the money create enduring impact.

1. Wilhelm, "Guerrilla Giving," lines 1–17.

The finding of free cash brightens a person's day, but their funds are randomly strewn to the wind in a fatalistic hope that they will reap productivity. This is a stark example of what we do when we give with only good intentions. Giving isn't as fun or easy as it appears. A strategic approach to giving—whatever the amount one gives—is essential.

While we can learn effective techniques that make for great grantmaking, it is only as givers assess and determine their own particular giving platform that the sector will be enriched. A review of the scope, competitive advantage, and logic behind others' philanthropic agendas will help each person arrive at their own giving niche.

It's not enough to just develop a plan—it must be implemented. While many foundations claim to have a strategy for their giving, a recent report suggests only a small number of grantmakers actually operate their foundations with a strategic process. Only eleven of forty-two foundation executives and program officers interviewed for a 2007 study by the Center for Effective Philanthropy defined their philanthropy as beginning with a strategic framework.[2] There is a significant gap between what people say and what is lived out.

One of the most telling indicators of whether a giver has a strategy is to assess whether there have been any potential grants that she found personally appealing but declined because it did not fit the defined giving strategy. Frequently, giving—even by major funders—is done on a whim, based on personal preference or relationship, and in reaction to the many appealing approaches being made. Defining strategy and committing to it, therefore, will not only assist a giver in giving more intentionally, but it will provide the conceptual framework with which to make giving decisions.

The same study classified givers by four groups: charitable bankers, perpetual adjusters, partial strategists, and total strategists.[3] Charitable bankers deploy their gifts with a transactional approach with the main goal of getting money out the door. Perpetual adjusters are attracted to new causes and change track frequently with every new trend. Partial strategists are guided by a strategic vision for their grantmaking, but allow for flexibility to seize unusual opportunities outside their main focus. Finally, total strategists develop a deep commitment to their purpose, and avoid any worthy causes that detract from their underlying commitment.

2. Bolduc et al., *Beyond the Rhetoric*, 10.

3. Ibid., 2–3.

Structure and process

The value of strategy and a deeper role for participatory philanthropy has increasing importance the further one moves along this continuum. As we matured in our grantmaking experience, we abandoned being a charitable banker and moved towards being partial strategists. It's likely that many endowed funds also follow a similar pattern as it becomes clear over time that strategic granting is both more rewarding and effective, and that the charitable banking model leaves much to be desired.

Conversations for your pilgrimage

1. Where are you on the strategy continuum?
2. If you have been giving for a long period, do you see your strategy evolving over time? How?

7

The need for structure

Mandata (Day 6)

Sunday dawned early, especially since the previous evening's festivities were barely winding down in the street before we were ready to set off. Spaniards love to party all night every weekend. I had slept poorly because my bunk was beside an open window—all night long music and laughter from a raucous party ebbed and flowed until the morning's light broke the spell.

Jaffer and I collected our thoughts and referred to guidebooks over espressos and croissants at a café on the square. We would move on today and hopefully reach our next destination by mid-afternoon.

Compared to yesterday's exertions, today's walk seemed easier—but that was only by comparison. It was still a tough slog. The terrain kept changing— sometimes tertiary roads paved with asphalt, other times muddy single-lane paths with thorny vegetation crowding over the trail. We started by following a small creek that burbled along the industrial blight at the edge of town, and then once again moved up into the pine-forested mountains. The side of the mountain had been blown away as a quarry for construction purposes.

After a few hours we finally emerged from the woods into a village that proudly declared its Basque identity with a sign posted by the town council. It affirmed we were in Spanish-occupied territory and that the only flag that would fly here was the Basque flag that looked strangely like a Union Jack that had been photoshopped with red, green, and white.

We were sipping coffees, observing the Sunday cyclists speeding around a dangerous corner, when we saw fellow pilgrims Elena and Sergio approaching.

This effervescent couple were from the Canary Islands, a province of Spain off the coast of Morocco, and like us, were walking the Camino del Norte. Elena emphatically insisted we should avoid Gernika as today's endpoint—it was rumored that the albergue our guidebooks recommended had closed. Instead, she suggested we find a newly opened albergue which was just a few kilometers off the camino prior to Gernika. We left them to get their own coffees, but with this helpful information, promised we would try to meet them at this new place.

Two hours later, Jaffer and I came to a sign pointing up an asphalt road that stated that our objective was one kilometer away. We began trekking upwards. The distance was undoubtedly longer than advertised, and every uphill turn of the road was disappointing. Finally we reached the top of the ridge, and found the new albergue as promised. It was a much needed oasis of rest for our weariness. In time, we were pleased to be joined by Elena and Sergio for the evening.

ARTAPE ATERPETXEA
Elejalde Auzoa, 7
Telf.: 94 625 72 04
48382 MENDATA
BIZKAIA

The randomness of Guerrilla Giving is a blatant example of how easy it is to be loose and unstrategic with one's giving. Yet we also began our grantmaking journey with haphazard grantmaking that was unrelated to a broader strategy. It was subject to random events, our own whims and fancies, as well as to outside pressures from persistent and compelling fundraisers.

In 1999, the coffee city of Armenia, Colombia was struck by a sudden and devastating earthquake. This region was close to our hearts—Karen and I had lived and worked nearby in the early 1990s, and our former colleagues, Rubén and Bev Ramírez, had started a vibrant church in that city. Grieved by the disaster, my father and I made a spur-of-the-moment decision to jump on a plane to visit our friends to see how we could best help.

Rubén drove us through street after street of collapsed buildings and we witnessed the damage that rendered their own new church completely unusable. Our friends themselves had been evicted from their damaged home, and had moved in with another church family. At the conclusion of the trip, my father was moved to offer our help, and at a café table, sketched out a financial plan on a napkin. We committed to beginning construction of a new facility. Through our connections, it would later be matched and completed by the generosity of a Canadian church.

We had no process for our giving, no way to monitor the six-figure grant in any way beyond the trust we had placed in our friends. We pledged funds to them blindly. When we committed the money, we did so without seeing architectural drawings for the proposed facility, and the planned construction was pay-as-you-go. Even the charity that received the grant was not set up for emergency funding, and we would likely be offside of relevant tax authority guidelines if we undertook such a venture today.

In this unique case, we were fortunate, although it wasn't easy. There were unexpected variances to the plan given the unstable and chaotic situation on the ground, but our friends exhibited the utmost integrity and commitment to fulfilling their plan. After a couple of years, the Colombians eventually constructed a large and beautiful sanctuary with multipurpose facilities which are still being used by the congregation. But from our end, we quickly learned that our philanthropy needed a structure and systems with which to operate. Without them, next time we weren't likely to be as fortunate.

While the first formal approach to a foundation is frequently made through the submission of a written concept paper, there are often preliminary conversations between potential partners that are less formal and more esoteric. These interactions can be helpful to float possible avenues for engagement, to assess the nature of projects being contemplated, and to determine whether the two partners could potentially work together.

Some foundations have a process in place that allows for these informal dialogues to occur. We've experimented with a few different means to accomplish this goal. In the past, our general approach was to meet with anyone who called and wanted to have coffee. We also advertised workshops with potential grantees at which they were informed in person of the foundation's priorities, and were given an opportunity to dialogue publicly. Potential grantees are frequently spread across a wide geographical area, so we have also scheduled webinars to share our priorities. Most recently, we have been experimenting with face-to-face meetings that are booked in advance on our website. (In order to not overwhelm myself, I set aside one day per month for these meetings, which are booked back-to-back in fifty-minute intervals over the course of the day.)

These advance meetings may seem burdensome to grantmakers, but they are truly important to achieve the mission of the foundation. The work of a foundation is more than grantmaking. It can also influence charities through an emphasis on best practices and setting solid standards, as well as insisting on creative, fundable projects. This best happens through face-to-face relationship rather than through a written submission.

Probably the most intangible thing that happens at this stage is developing an awareness of potential positive chemistry between the organization and the grantmaker. Are they on the same page? Are the missional objectives of both parties aligned? Could there be a relationship of trust? First impressions and the gut check that intuition provides is often what makes or breaks an eventual partnership.

Unfortunately, most foundations don't have the capacity to meet with potential partners prior to a concept paper being delivered. Most partners have to rely on materials available online and engaging with existing networks of people in the know to understand a specific foundation's mission.

Conversations for your pilgrimage

1. Is your grantmaking haphazard and random, or have you developed a process to guide your charitable giving?

2. Are you open to conversations with charities as you implement your philanthropic plan?

8

Formal but flexible processes

Eskerika (Day 7)

This morning dawned bright. After a week of clouds, today was the first sunny day, and the sun glistened off the fog lifting from the mountains. My body seemed to be adapting to the rhythms of this disciplined journey. As a result, my walk was inspiring and not arduous; I felt light. Jaffer and I trekked downhill for the first two hours, with exceptional views of Gernika in the valley as we descended.

Gernika has had a tragic history. During the Spanish Civil War, Franco's Nationalist forces were not retaining Basque loyalty. He allied with Hitler to help him vanquish the Basques, which the Luftwaffe used to pioneer a new style of air warfare called saturation bombing. In 1937 the Germans strafed the town in an unexpected and merciless attack. As the townspeople gathered their belongings to flee the city, the air force returned for a second round, and mercilessly obliterated civilians in the streets.

Pablo Picasso memorialized this heinous act with a painting, Gernika, which hangs today at the Reina Sofía in Madrid. I've seen a copy of this painting displayed at the United Nations in New York. It reminds us of the evils that occur when warfare mentality and industrial might collude.

Last night Jaffer pledged with our small group to make tonight's meal at the albergue in Eskerika. The rudimentary, rural hostel, located ten kilometers beyond the city, provided only bunk beds and showers, and no food. In order to eat, we had to carry our own food with us to cook in the communal kitchen.

Structure and process

As we drank our coffees in Gernika, we noticed an open-air market was setting up across from the plaza. We wandered the aisles picking out fresh produce—green beans, onions, garlic, tomatoes, fresh bread, and a lemon—then located a supermarket for the dry goods: lentils, rice, spices, and a bottle of Rioja. We divided up the goods and rearranged our backpacks, which had become considerably heavier, and continued onward.

As we left the city, we chanced upon Elena and Sergio with whom we had planned to eat that evening. They informed us they were slowing their pace and wouldn't join us for dinner. I was proud of Jaffer for rolling with the unexpected news—we had just purchased a lot of food for the whole group, which was weighing down our packs, but he didn't complain.

Why was it that the last stop of the day always seemed to require a final ascent? In the afternoon heat, we hiked up the rural landscape, gasping with each breath. Finally, in the middle of nowhere, we arrived just as the albergue opened at three to receive new guests. After showering and laundry, Jaffer began cooking and within an hour a fantastic Indian meal of curry and dal was plated. We invited two hungry stragglers to join us. Apart from an early morning croissant, this was our first food of the day, and we felt like we had earned every mouthful.

Generally accepted approaches to foundations often require a two-stage written approach, something we soon adopted. The first stage is a preliminary overview of the project requiring support known as a concept paper, letter of inquiry, or executive summary. We often abbreviate this to LOI, or Letter of Inquiry. This brief document, often just two pages in length, highlights the main points of the reasons for seeking partnership and reviews how the project will be fulfilled through it.

Developing a concept paper requires a level of rigor and introduces discipline of thought and planning into the potential project, improving its viability. The potential partner is asked to briefly develop their case for the foundation's involvement.

Many grantseekers have the impression that the critical juncture lies much later in the process, when the official committee that reviews and accepts new grants makes their decision. But this is incorrect. In the majority of cases, only a small percentage of applications that make it to the committee table are declined. In other words: if an application makes it through the LOI stage, the likelihood of obtaining a grant is greatly improved. Of course, this will vary widely depending on each foundation's process.

It's often at the LOI stage where the tough decisions are made, and it's the staff who make them. This seemingly simple, two-page *précis* is the gateway to a potential grant, and it's accompanied by other behind-the-scenes activity that might not be apparent to the grantseeker.

When it's time to assess LOIs, we review them to determine how well they match with the foundation's grantmaking agenda. Each organization's web page is explored. Financial information for the past few fiscal years is researched using online tools such as Canada's CRA charity database or the USA's GuideStar. If the organization has a history with the foundation, the caliber and success of past grants is also reviewed. A phone call or two may be made to other donors who have experience with the applicant. These steps generally give us enough information to identify whether or not the applicant's priorities and the grantmaker's are aligned.

Only a small percentage of LOIs make it through to a full application. A foundation's ability to connect with the public and to communicate their mission can be gauged by the percentage of LOIs that are declined at this stage. Frequently, there seems to be a disconnect between what the foundation aspires to do, and public perception of the foundation's mission. If a grantmaker receives many applications unrelated to their philanthropic purpose, they should reconsider how adequately they are communicating its mission, process, and aims.

At times, however, charities themselves are deficient in matching their goals with the philanthropist's. Investing in research is key. As challenging as it is, grantseekers must get to know their potential donors. While it frequently isn't possible in the conventional sense of meeting face to face, there are ways to learn grantmaker priorities. One can investigate past successful grants on the foundation's (and their charity partners') websites, use other online tools, look for trends in their granting, and seek insight as to where they are heading in the future. As well, if the foundation's principals blog or interact with the public through social media, this allows ready access to personality and interests. Following these interactions can offer clues to the foundation's future interests and the passions that drive decision-making. Other successful grant recipients can be interviewed to determine what drove their success. It is important to emphasize current priorities. Old blog posts, grants from the past, or obsolete public statements from many years ago may no longer be valid indicator of current donor intent. Foundations can and do change their publicly stated priorities.

It is imperative that private foundations are transparent so that charities can understand their grantmaking priorities—the more foundations hide their colors or have ill-defined purposes, the greater the volume of requests inconsistent with the philanthropic goals of the foundation. This becomes a distressing waste of time for both grantmaker and grantseeker.

Foundations develop an application process to ascertain that potential grantee projects are aligned with the organizational mission of the funder. As well, to comply with the foundation's charitable purpose and legal standards, it is essential to have on file a detailed explanation of how funds are being deployed for charitable purposes.

Foundations need to ascertain what parts of their application process are essential to giving good grants, and which are superfluous. At times, information sought in an application is readily available on the organization's web page. If the organization is a previous grantee to a foundation, does the foundation already have a file with the same information that is being requested? If so, attempts should be made to simplify the complexity of the application.

Laborious applications are not ideal. The multiplicity of complicated application processes for foundation and corporate grants has created such a heavy workload that outside professionals are often paid to research and write grant applications on behalf of charities, spawning a whole industry of grant writing.

Simplifying the application process does not mean funding carelessly. Organizations seeking partnership with donors of all sizes need to be clear about their case for support. This is most helpfully articulated when meaningful indicators are developed. Baseline indicators reveal the place an organization is starting from, and divulge the rationale for the charity's intervention. Milestones are developed that reflect what can be expected at various points in the grant's evolution. Final reports will name the tangible accomplishments made through the course of the grant.

In an application, defining inputs, outputs, outcomes, and desired impact is one approach to articulating the activities and goals for a project. Results-based management (RBM) is used by many government agencies and larger charities to help quantify what funding is actually accomplishing through grants that are made. This technical approach breaks down the project into bite-sized components. Their approach can be tedious for charities, but also instructive.

Inputs are the pieces required to launch: human resources, time, money, tools. To run a daily after-school homework assistance program in a high-rise tower for twenty immigrant teenagers, for instance, an organization might require a half-time trained staff person, three volunteers offering two hours per day, four computers, Internet access, supplies, snacks, heating, electricity, and books. Perhaps there's a budget of $20,000 for the eight months that school is in session.

Outputs are the actual physical results of the intervention. In our example, this could be an average of eighteen students attending over the course of the year, several youths offering a specific number of volunteer hours, and a specific number of hours of administrative oversight done by the director of the program.

Outcomes describe how the intervention has directly benefited the recipients during the course of the project. Possible outcomes in this scenario could be that the average grade of assisted students increased by 4 percent from the previous year, that skipped classes were reduced by 18 percent, and that the average satisfaction levels of the teens' integration into the school have improved by 15 percent.

Impact reflects the long-term consequences of a project. While various factors beyond the actual project may influence consequences, consciously attempting to determine an organization's impact allows for focused programming. In this case, the impact could be a 24 percent increase in the number of immigrant teens who are accepted into a university from the local school being assisted through the homework program. The impact of a grant will often take years to achieve, and organizations must be cautious about interpreting data as being solely a result of their intervention.

Grantseekers should pay attention to what the application is requesting, as this often gives significant clues to the priorities of the grantmaker. For example, in a common application we use, we request the grantseeker define how their project hopes to be sustainable in the future years following our exit from funding. This indicates the grantmaker does not see us as an annual ongoing source of revenue, and ensures that plans to continue the program must rely on others or on earned income generated from the project.

Unfortunately, each private funder creates their own forms, systems, and timelines for reporting back. This causes grief to potential partners who must spend hours using each foundation's customized forms to apply for support. One of our priorities with my new organization, Stronger Philanthropy, is to be a hub for granting with several different foundations using a single, streamlined application system. This eases the process for charities, and the same application can then be considered by participating groups of grantmakers.

The written application may seem to involve a tedious process, but it also creates the discipline for a conscious and intentional development of project goals and holds the charity to account for what they themselves say they will do. But pixelated words on a computer screen only go so far in determining whether a project is viable or not. At this stage, the foundation's due diligence process needs to flesh out the reality behind the words and numbers as presented. The process continues with an in-person site visit.

Conversations for your pilgrimage

1. Have you developed a structured approach to grantmaking that best serves your family's priorities? What is it?

2. How could you streamline your application process to align with other grantmakers?

9

The power of site visits

Bilbao (Day 8)

Under overcast skies we began walking once again, a twenty-five-kilometer day ahead of us, to reach the edgy and unconventional city of Bilbao. We walked from rural isolation to urban postmodernity in eight hours.

At the first café where we fueled up on espressos, I realized I needed to make a critical decision. When we approached our breakfast stop, Jaffer and I happened to reunite with yesterday's dinner companions, and as it turned out we would end up walking with them into the city. The elder of these two companions seemed to suck up all the atmosphere around us with his expansive ego and outrageous opinions. He needed a platform and an audience—and he had apparently chosen us to feed that need. After walking for eight days, my exhaustion left me at the threshold of tolerance. It had been two days since this character had attached himself to us, and for my own sanity, I had to take remedial action. If I didn't act decisively, I feared he would walk alongside us all the way to Santiago.

We trudged through industrial towns surrounding the Basque capital, past stark, utilitarian factories and under graffiti-covered bridges. Finally, the last challenge came in the heat of the day: for the last seven kilometers we faced a 500-meter rise to a ridge and then a final, steep descent into Bilbao.

At the top, panting, we looked at a map mounted on a pedestal overlooking the city. The others declared their intention to find lodging at the official albergue on the far edge of the city. This was my moment: I stated I had other plans. I was going to take a rest day to explore Bilbao, and in particular the

Frank Gehry-designed Guggenheim Museum located along its river. I would find lodging in the center of the old town and stay there two nights. Jaffer, seeing a way out of a sticky situation, quickly agreed with me. We said goodbye, wishing them well, and moved on ahead.

Great cities have great museums. Bilbao has the Guggenheim, and surprisingly, Winnipeg has a dramatic, new Museum for Human Rights. A few years ago, I traded warm spring rains in Toronto for minus-30-degree wind chill in Winnipeg. Though sunny, the frigid, prairie air sliced through my clothes. But the ice outside was melted by a site visit which revealed the unexpected passion of a new organization.

Siloam Mission was a new organization to me. Before I laid eyes on this mission in the downtown core, I had only general impressions informed through a website, an application, and a review of their financial statements. While these were generally positive, the archaic-sounding name turned me off and I imagined a stereotypical inner-city ministry much like many I have toured in the past, an organization that survived by the skin of its teeth through skimping and saving resources.

Their paperwork contradicted my imaginings. The application spoke of rapid growth—from two to thirty-five staff in five years, and from a budget barely enough to support one staff person to an operating budget of seven digits. I was intrigued and wondered how this had been possible.

Upon arrival at Princess Street, the first thing I noticed was the building. I'm not often wowed by charity structures. But I noticed that Winnipeg has a fair share of great industrial buildings—century-old, factory-like structures, four or five stories high, lots of brick and stone, huge windows. And 300 Princess was a gem stuck on the wrong side of the tracks. If I were an architect, I would say it had great bones. This old skeleton came complete with a spine: an immense, rattletrap elevator, big enough for a forklift, with an accordion door that ascended four floors to access more than 55,000 square feet of space. And miraculously, the old bones of industry had been given new life by compassion for the less fortunate.

In this center, over the previous year, more than 112,000 meals had been served, 1,500 food hampers delivered, 6,400 pieces of clothing distributed, and 20,000 volunteer hours offered. It was obvious that some significant outreach was being accomplished. But the best thing was the linking that was being done between the compassionate and the less fortunate in the city.

The executive director began to tell me their story. A wealthy Winnipegger had died, and, in a bold act of benevolence, had left the bulk of his considerable estate to "the homeless of the city." The executor of his will put out a call for proposals from community organizations, and to everyone's great surprise, Siloam—at the time a small grassroots charity—became the beneficiary of a seven-figure gift.

Walking through the mission, I could see what this gift had wrought: contractors, builders, painters, and drywallers were everywhere. Every floor of the building was abuzz with construction as new walls, electrical outlets, pipes, and flooring emerged to produce a huge new shelter for 105 homeless people, a medical clinic with five exam rooms along with rooms for dentists and a chiropractor, and some administrative space. In a few years, Siloam had become the main service provider to Winnipeg's homeless population—over a hundred people sat chatting, sleeping, or eating in the welcome center as I walked through.

It was only by actually walking through on a site visit that I witnessed a deeply sobering reality: more than 80 percent of the individuals who receive services are First Nations peoples. I experienced for myself that this was a place of warmth, care, food, and rest. The atmosphere and the way staff and volunteers interacted with their guests conferred dignity. The big broad prairie windows, sun streaming in, painted a different face on homelessness that I would never have seen without a site visit. The importance of this shelter became even clearer when I had to exit back into the minus-thirty-degree weather outside.

Site visits are about more than a physical walk-through or an experience, though these are important. It's also the moment to have niggling doubts confirmed or eliminated through questioning or observation. It's a moment to have your heart moved.

I prepare for my site visit with a list of questions or concerns about the organization, its leadership and the proposed project. I need to look the executive director in the eyes and assess her ability to deliver; I need to assess my own ability to enter into a granting relationship without reservation.

Structure and process

Many times my jaundiced opinions have been softened through a site visit; at other times, red flags were raised during interviews that prevented me from wholeheartedly endorsing the proposed project to our grantmakers.

Conversations for your pilgrimage

1. Do you visit potential grant recipients and view their work first hand? Why or why not?

2. What processes would you need to develop if you made this a standard part of your grantmaking?

10

Dashboard indicators

La Arena (Day 9)

The day off in Bilbao was a welcome oasis in the midst of this challenging journey. I was not in shape for these relentless days of walking and my exhaustion was taking a toll. The Guggenheim did not disappoint, and its quirky creativity fed my soul. A chance encounter that evening also made my day.

Jaffer and I were seated at a crowded outdoor café in Plaza Berria, preparing to order items for dinner when an explosion erupted at the next table over where a Spanish couple with two small children were seated. The little three-year-old girl was having a tantrum. She kicked the table leg, jostling the aluminum table, and a wine glass slid off, the ball of the glass catching the seat of a chair on the way down. In a perfect arc only a physicist could anticipate, the liquid soared over our heads and landed the next table over, the glass crashing into smithereens. It was such a perfect, slow-motion chain reaction, that I found it comical, and burst out laughing. But what came next made it more comical.

Within seconds, a Dutch couple arrived, blithely unaware of the drama, even though they were stepping on broken glass. There were no empty tables left in the café, so the tourists asked in their broken Spanish if they could join the family at their table. Their timing was abysmal. The small girl was sobbing and her embarrassed parents were attempting to clean up glass along with a frustrated, angry waiter. Language was a barrier, and I saw how the Dutch couple were oblivious, so I beckoned them over to our table. They gratefully accepted, and immediately sat down. From the moment they pulled up their chairs, it was like we were old friends. Embarrassment and high drama brought us together. We sat and laughed, conversing about life, faith, work, and family for two hours. It was a beautiful moment of grace that snuck up and surprised us with new friendships.

Jaffer and I left Bilbao behind the next morning on our ninth day of walking. We decided to choose the less complicated, alternate route which hugged the eastern edge of the Rio Nervión that flowed northward into the Atlantic. At some point we knew we had to cross the river as the camino to Santiago continued westward. While our guidebooks and apps showed us that this alternate trail was possible, it didn't reveal how we would cross—and a search on Google Maps confusingly showed there was no bridge, just open water all the way to the sea.

Perplexed, I stopped a bread delivery van and asked the driver how we could keep going. As a Bilbao native, he proudly raved about the solution: a unique suspension tram had been built in the late nineteenth century by a protégé of Gustav Eiffel. It shuttled small cars and pedestrians from one bank to the other. The tram car hung over the river suspended by cables, and was not an obstruction for large ships passing below.

Most of today was bleak, urban walking through graffitied port lands, but eventually we began to enter areas with less density. Leaving the urban areas, a huge network of paved walking and biking trails became our camino, and it was smooth sailing toward the coast. La Arena emerged, a small, gritty beach town, and the smell of salt relaxed our weary muscles with the first whiff.

A comprehensive way to discern charity health is through a dashboard tool, an analytical, graphic framework that assists us in making a thoughtful and comprehensive evaluation of an organization's health when we are considering partnerships.[1] Our dashboard indicators allow for a quick summary of organizational health on a single page, and generates a score that

---

1. We currently make the results of this comprehensive dashboard tool available to clients who request Stronger Philanthropy's due diligence services.

generally indicates to our grantmaking committee whether we will should proceed with a grant for the organization. As well, it introduces a measure of discipline to our grantmaking that, used consistently, begins to provide a means of evaluating one organization against another.

Sources we use for completing our dashboard include the organization's readily available online financial data for the last complete fiscal year, data from the application to the foundation, historical data from past grants (if any), and input from a site visit.

There are five major areas of interest to us in determining an organization's health: financial, development, accountability, leadership, and mission. We generate scores in each of these areas and then average the five scores to create a total score for each applicant charity. I'll review the evaluation system below.

Financial

It's easy to become distracted by reams of financial data, but we distill an organization's financial reality into a few concrete indicators. We paint the financial picture of an organization using data gathered from an organization's two most recent audited financial statements. If audited statements don't exist, we refer to online data published by government authorities for all charities. However, as having third-party audited statements is one of the prerequisites for our grantmakers, this scenario is rare.

The following are our indicators:

- Growth rate: We believe growth is healthy and that effective philanthropy rewards growth with further investment. We assess how quickly an organization is expanding by charting growth in income over the past three years. Declines in income are given a score of zero. However, too rapid growth could indicate potential danger zones if the organization has not built infrastructure to handle the inflow.

- Months of unrestricted fund rate: This indicator tracks the unrestricted fund balance divided by the total monthly required overhead. How many months worth of unrestricted funds does the organization have available for operations in the event of a crisis? A rule of thumb would be to seek three months of available funding. Having this type of unrestricted funding available internally allows for management to make decisions without immediate pressures.

- Working capital rate: Dividing current assets by the current liabilities offers an organization's rate of liquidity. Organizations that score well in this indicator will have a rate of two-to-one. Again, a positive score for liquidity indicates that an organization is able to operate effectively without the immediate stresses of bills owing.

- Overhead rate: The final financial indicator assesses the amount of funds spent on overhead. All expenses for administration and development are divided by the total expenses. Care should be taken when assessing overhead, with 80:20 being the rule of thumb that is promoted by the charities directorate as a guide.

It is important to realize that organizations in stages of aggressive growth will require more overhead in their expansion efforts, while organizations with low overhead costs may not be professionally run, so a high or a low overhead may not adequately reflect health in and of itself. Also, how an organization assesses what are administrative or development expenses is an ongoing issue for debate, with organizations having variable approaches to accounting for what is program and what is overhead.

Many other potential indicators could be used to determine financial health, but we have found these four reveal important factors which we consider when determining financial health. We've found it to be important not to only look at the numbers, but to drill down to the story behind them as indicators may be high or low due to some unusual event that is justifiable.

Development

A charity's degree of organizational health is dependent on a well-structured, thoughtful approach to fundraising. Various strategies are operative, but a generalized observation is that the larger and more mature the organization, the greater the likelihood of its reliance on smaller donors and a mass marketing plan. A large supportive group of small donors is the backbone of good charity management, and most organizations desire to grow this area effectively.

Some start-up organizations, for a while at least, structure their initial growth around a major donor development plan. Having a few strong investors at the front end helps to get an organization up and running, but they should also have a plan for broadening their donor base over time to allow for ongoing sustainability.

The following four areas help to define an overall rating for an organization's fundraising ability:

- Major donor dependency rate: Valuating the top ten donations to an organization over the past fiscal year shows the degree of an organization's reliance on its major donors for annual sustainability. In our application process, we request the amounts of the top ten donations received by the organization in the past fiscal year. Dividing this amount by the annual income reveals the percentage an organization is reliant on these top ten donors. Included in this figure are all donations made by government sources and major individual or foundation donors. Privacy laws prevent disclosure of individual donor names, but governments, churches or other charities, and private or public foundations should be listed, as their donations are part of the public record. Knowing the top ten donations is frequently helpful information in our due diligence process, as we can follow up with other major donors as to the effectiveness of their partnership with an organization. It also helps us to know how best to position our grant for an organization. Do we want to be in the top ten or would we prefer to contribute to a lesser degree?

- Fundraising strategy score: We assess an organization's fundraising plan and score it between one and ten. Who will they approach for funding this year? Who are their major partners? How do they broaden their strategy to include smaller individual donors? What is their mass fundraising strategy? Does it include mass mailings? If so, how many per year and what is the average income from this effort? Alternatively, is their fundraising merely a come-what-may approach not based on any integrated strategy? A well-developed plan with a thoughtful, disciplined approach by dedicated development staffing will pay off in the long run for an organization. An essential part of development effort involves a personal, customized approach to major donors.

- Marketing score: Relevant, appealing organizational marketing positions an organization among its competitors, as well as clearly communicates mission, vision, program objectives, and impact. An annual report is frequently the best document to clarify how an organization presents itself. We look at samples of websites, brochures, and other marketing materials and assess how frequently these tools are updated.

- Authenticity score: For lack of a better term, we assess what may be termed "authenticity." What we look for here is a humble organization that has a realistic perspective of itself and its work in its donor development. It seeks partnerships, and plays a role in the broader nonprofit world, recognizing it cannot act in isolation. Organizations that present themselves as having all the answers and work without relying on others are those that would not typically benefit from the types of partnerships we are seeking.

Accountability

The need for transparency and accountability to the public and to donors is increasing as attention is placed on charities to prove public benefit. As a result, a few years ago, we introduced this separate category in order to rank charities in this area. The following scores combine to provide a measure of an organization's public accountability:

- Financial statements score: It's becoming increasingly common practice for charities to post their audited financial statements online in an easily found area of their website. We consider this a best practice to be emulated for transparency's sake. However, not all auditors are equal. Not all chartered accountants have experience with nonprofits, and so charity boards and CEOs should insist their auditor liaise with organizations such as Imagine Canada or the Canadian Council of Christian Charities to determine how best to present audited information for charities.

- Accessibility score: This subjective score is high when we find organizations that have accessible, vulnerable, open leaders, who are a joy to work with, and who are transparent even with bad news. Alternatively, an organization would rank low if interactions are forced and contrived, we have to dig for information, bad news is covered up, and/or they are hard to reach.

- Reporting score: Good reporting is one way that allows us as grant-makers to determine whether we are achieving our mission. Comprehensive, attractive, compelling annual and project reports circle back to communicate to funders the value and impact of their grants. Late reporting or inferior reports merit a lower score.

- Digital media score: We assess the relevance and appeal of the organization's digital presence for web and social media. Does the website invite comments or have a feedback mechanism allowing online conversations with donors and other interested parties? Is the website current? An online presence also needs to include the development of a social media presence, particularly if the organization is interested in reaching out to newer donors and a younger constituency. Is there an organizational Facebook page? Do they use Twitter? Do they contribute to online forums? Does the executive director have a current and engaging blog? This type of social engagement is expected in relevant charities, is sought after by Millennials, and leads toward a measure of public accountability.

Leadership

An organization's leaders set the culture, determine the strategic plan, and drive forward toward mission fulfillment. A healthy leadership culture is therefore essential. To develop a score for leadership, we measure board governance, CEO competency, strategic plan, and the management team.

- Board governance score: Knowing who is on an organization's board is revealing, as is learning who has recently gone off a board and why. How does the board operate? How often do they meet? Is the board comprised of diverse individuals bringing a variety of skills and insights to the board table? How do they view their role in relationship to the executive director? We look for an independent board of professional women and men who monitor and strategically guide the organization's ongoing service, and hold the CEO accountable for his or her actions according to an agreed-upon strategic plan. I know of one organization whose board meets monthly, where the staff and board members meet without distinction of roles, and where the board is heavily involved in the daily operations of the charity—board and management lines have been blurred, and the effectiveness of good governance has been reduced. Other organizations' boards meet only once a year; their roles are mere tokenism. Both examples are extremes of poor governance.

- Executive director score: The success of an organization rises and falls on its main leader. Is this a person who can be trusted to lead this organization? What education and experience does she bring to the job? How recently has this individual arrived in his role? An apparent trend is seeing the CEO hired from outside an organization with a background in the private or corporate sector. While this appears to be a good strategy, we also recognize that the aspiration of an entrepreneur to do good through leading a charity is often not enough to bridge the culture gap between the for-profit and charitable sectors.

- Strategic plan score: Does an organization follow a written strategic plan? How was it developed? How is it being used? We seek to know to what extent an organization's daily operations are aligned to this strategy, and whether it is shared by both the board and the staff. Frequently we find that a strategic plan is either abandoned on a shelf, or is referred to by a limited group of people within an organization. It has not taken on an inspirational, guiding role for all members of an entire organization.

- Management team score: Who is on the management team? What are their strengths? When was the last transition out of or onto the team? We look for diversity and complementary skills, and seek to uncover a collegial mutuality among the team—or, alternatively, to determine if there is an environment of mistrust. It is important to assess whether there are financial and accounting skills available to the team through one or more members of the senior leadership. Frequently in smaller charities, staff with core competencies in program delivery are promoted to positions of leadership, and flounder with the responsibilities linked to financial and management oversight.

Mission

The fifth area for our review relates to the organizational mission, which reflects on the relevancy and impact of what they do:

- Focus score: We assess an organization's ability to focus on a specific area, to develop a niche by which it is known and in which it has excelled. Some charities, particularly historic ones with a broad and unclear platform, have developed many different types of outreach over time. This is often driven by passionate individuals but has not been managed from the center. Other charities have taken time to say no to activities that take them far beyond their missional focus. Charities that have a clear, fresh focus merit a higher score in our system.

- Relevance score: A charity's relevance to its clients and the general public is also assessed. It would score higher when it demonstrates a profound awareness of the challenges it is addressing within its context, and has created a relevant response to these issues. Lower scores apply to those who have not taken time to become relevant to their context.

- Impact score: Though impact takes years to achieve, developing an organization that is concerned with its impact and measuring it over time is important to us. Such organizations have a defined, measurable impact, and telling stories of its impact is part of the culture.

- Capacity score: A final score is given which assesses an organization's capacity to achieve its mission. Does it have qualified personnel in place to achieve its goals? Does it have the infrastructure required? If it is questionable that an organization has adequate resources in place to achieve its goals, it would receive a lower score.

Many donors immediately jump to assess the viability of a project before taking the time to assess whether the framework can support it. Understanding the charity's capacity and organizational health is essential, and should always be the starting point before digging deeper to assess specific projects proposed by the charity.

Conversations for your pilgrimage

1. Do you agree that a healthy organization is needed for viable projects to be successful?

2. What tools or systems do you use to thoughtfully evaluate the organizations you are considering funding?

11

Assessing projects

Islares (Day 10)

Today we walked out of Basque Country, and entered into Cantabria, a less autonomously minded district of Spain. We crossed La Arena's beach on a boardwalk, passing some pilgrims who, due to limited albergue beds, had been forced to sleep on the sand overnight. As we approached an ascent of 200 stairs set in a cliff at Pobeña, we laughed with unexpected recognition at who we were about to overtake. It was Elena and Sergio, whom we had last seen a few days earlier. Both of them were the type of people to put a smile on my face—Sergio with his joking around, and Elena with her inquisitiveness and broad smile. Reaching the top, we walked along the naked cliff-edge with brilliant views of the crashing surf below. I looked up bolero music on YouTube, and using my smartphone as a miniature boom box, Sergio enthusiastically led us in singing retro Spanish classics as we ambled along the edge of the cliff.

After several hours, we descended to Castro Urdiales, a large beachside city, and stopped for an open-air lunch of freshly caught merluza and pulpo (whitefish and octopus). Sergio and Elena decided to call it quits for the day— the lure of the oceanside vacation vibe was tempting—but Jaffer and I wanted to push on to the next town. Around three, in the heat of the day, we arrived in Islares, the yellow arrows pointing us directly to the albergue just off the main road.

In hindsight, we wished we had stayed with Elena and Sergio. Islares wasn't much to write home about. This seasonal town relied on holidaymakers for its economy. It was strung along a main road ending at the ocean, and a couple of decrepit beachfront cafés and a sad camping area were all the services available.

The albergue itself was also less than spectacular. We were stacked three people high in two triple-bunk beds, comprised of wooden slats and two-inch foams, with one lucky guy (Jaffer) getting a single bed (a mattress on the floor). This added up to seven people in one small room; there were twelve next door. We met a Danish family with two sons slightly younger than mine, and an American woman from Cape Cod who thrashed around in the night letting fly her water bottle, camino guidebook, pen, and sleeping bag cover, all missiles which landed inches from my head on the bottom bunk. We had a good chuckle about it in the morning, although getting beaned by a full water bottle would not have been a pleasant way to be awakened.

I finally come to the area most of interest to donors in our due diligence process: the project proposed by an organization. This is the area that shows why the organization exists. It is what likely prompted the potential giver's interest in considering a project from the organization. However, a project's success is built on a strong framework of infrastructure that includes the aforementioned strengths of leadership, finances, development, account-ability, and mission. Projects will bloom and die quickly without the fertile soil of charity health that nourishes them.

When assessing a project, the following questions help us think through the proposed project more objectively:

- Clarity: Is the project clearly presented? Does it have a specific focus with measurable outcomes?

- Outcomes: What indicators have been developed to help the organiza-tion communicate its successes or failures back to the grantmaker?

- Coherence: Does the project make sense? Does it seem a reasonable pathway forward for the charity?

- Viability: How likely is it that the project will succeed? Are building blocks in place to ensure the organization will achieve this project?

- Sustainability: What measures are in place to ensure the project will survive after our contribution is completed? Will the project develop an earned revenue stream? If not, does the organization have strong fundraising capability to ensure the longevity of the project?

- Personnel: Do personnel have a track record of achieving project goals? Are they committed to this project?

- Relevance: Is the project a relevant response to the challenges being addressed?

- Transformation: This subjective area relates to that which intangibly occurs through great charitable activity, and is based on the assumption that meaningful outreach impacts not only the physical but also the heart. We ask: what type of meaningful change will occur in the lives of the target audience as a result of the program?[1]

- Chemistry: The most intangible criteria is this one, and it takes awareness of the grantmaker's priorities and personality. How well will this program fit with the culture of the grantmaker's family, foundation, or corporate social responsibility initiative? How does the program advance the giver's desire to contribute towards societal and cultural transformation?

A request may come from an organization that is financially sound, has solid leadership and an excellent development staff, but if the program holds no interest for the philanthropist, or if it doesn't have the right chemistry, it will be declined. These declinations are

---

1. Givers must make a judgment call as to what they value and how they define meaningful transformation. For some givers, investing in the arts and witnessing the inner joy that comes to audiences through artistic achievement is an aspect of transformation that is valued by a giver. In a different sort of program, perhaps one in which microfinancial services are offered to poor entrepreneurial women in the developing world, transformation is found in the dignity and respect clients gain through the programming. For religious givers, the gift of spiritual vitality is what is most important—an example could be programming that allows for a spiritual reorientation of one's life, which in turn produces a stronger, more rooted family life. These intangibles—the aesthetic, humanitarian, and the spiritual—are all vague yet necessary elements it's easy to overlook when assessing effective programming.

often the hardest to communicate back to the organization, but if saving the whales is not a priority for the grantmaker, the organization must learn their much-loved priorities are not the same as the giver's.

While a well-developed proposal does not guarantee whether or not a project will ultimately be a success, it does help to serve as a window on how the organization develops its ideas, markets them, and seeks to capture donations. Proposals can be so wordy that they lose the reader in the text, or they can be so vague that I sometimes wonder what they are actually planning on doing with the investment they hope we make. Watching how the proposal is delivered often allows for glimpses into whether the organization reads their potential donor correctly. Does the proposal focus on your stated priorities as a giver? Is it all marketing and little substance? We can often determine the quality of the proposal in the charity's ability to communicate the essence of the project.

After analyzing an organization's health using our dashboard system, and then assessing the project's viability, we take a deep breath, reflect, and pray—aware that numbers and metrics don't always tell the entire story.

One organization we support makes a significant difference in the world around them. As we analyze their organization, some of the metrics used to evaluate program success are positive, and encouragingly so. But when we pass their organization through our dashboard tool, they don't pass muster. This organization is a start-up that is still on the trajectory up towards sustainability. It takes time to become a healthy and mature charitable organization and we are patiently working with them to get there.

We have often struggled with the question: How do you compare charity x and charity y to develop meaningful statistics, given the varied nature of charitable activity and the variances in size and age of the charities being measured? While measurement can be frustrating and the results don't always tell the whole story, we strive to combine analysis with judgment, common sense, intuition, and thoughtful improvisation.

We welcome comments on our metrics and we continue to think about them; we are also wary of hyper-focusing on them. An excessive focus on metrics can put too much faith in the numbers. No one will ever know for sure how many people they're helping, or the ripple effect cascading through a charity's efforts. Assessing the viability of organizations involves literally hundreds of judgment calls.

A disciplined analysis, however, is still critically important, and we will continue to insist on the rigor of due diligence. We often turn down opportunities to partner with charities due to abnormalities in their metrics. Perhaps their unrestricted fund balance is in negative territory, indicating restricted funds may have been used outside their intended purpose. Perhaps they demonstrate that over time they are shrinking, not expanding. Perhaps they prove that they already have excessive assets available for the project, and don't really need our money. At the same time, we recognize that our due diligence process is a framework with which to begin a conversation, not end it. We remember it is a tool, but it's only one of the tools in the philanthropist's toolbox.

Conversations for your pilgrimage

1. How do you determine whether a project is worth funding and likely to be successful?

2. What type of assessment process could you create to open up conversations for decision-making amongst your board or family?

12

Making grant decisions

Santoña (Day 11)

Though it was just six o'clock, my day had once again begun. I quickly dressed and joined other pilgrims for breakfast—a baguette with hazelnut-chocolate spread, and black coffee. Jaffer and I were out the door by 6:30; there was no reason to linger.

We hiked along the N-634, a secondary highway that is intertwined with the camino all along the northern coast. There were pluses and minuses to this scenario. It was easier walking on flat pavement. But buses and trucks whizzed by perilously close, and the concrete was hard on the feet after several consecutive hours.

As we had the day before, we arrived in a large beachfront city, this one called Laredo. I spotted a hardware store, and popped in to purchase a small switchblade. For several days after my camino stick was gifted to me from "San Antonio del Bosque," I had walked with it, green and unpeeled. Antonio had suggested I get a knife and peel it, and then, after a few months of drying, varnish it. I looked forward to this memento of my journey.

We moved through the large town at midday. The sun cooked us as we plodded forward along the promenade, and we felt overdressed in our camino gear next to the bathing-suit-clad Spaniards. After over an hour we arrived at the end of the peninsula with nothing ahead but salt water. Our guidebook informed us we could find a boat to take us across the short passage to Santoña on the western shore. On inquiring, a man indicated a small group of people standing in the sand. We trudged over to join them, and presently a

*rickety boat appeared. We boarded, paying two euros for the passage. Acid
rock incongruously blared from cheap speakers anchored to the wheelhouse.*

*Within a few minutes we had docked in Santoña, and in the first major
plaza of the town, we found an* albergue *that would suit us for the night. After
a long lunch and a much-needed* siesta, *I stole away to peel my stick on a
bench. It became a mesmerizing moment for contemplation as two local boys
watched me, fascinated.*

The final aspect of due diligence involves coming to some conclusions
which will be presented to the decision-makers. In a narrative report, we
record our past history with the organization, a description of the site visit,
a list of pros and cons related to the project, and then a list of several options for the grantmaking committee to assist in their decision-making.
They either choose one of the listed options, or at times create their own
response to the proposal.

Sometimes it becomes clear that the project is not well designed, that
there are gaps in the plan, or that an organization is really not a good fit for
the donor. At other times, my mind has shifted significantly from a less-
than-positive review to an awareness that perhaps our funding could make
a meaningful and strategic difference. Regardless, my recommendation to
the grantmaker will be backed up with a rationale based on the due diligence process.

My greatest joy comes when I can announce, based on effective due
diligence, that a grant is forthcoming and a partnership will be established
between grantmaker and grantseeker. While we announce all approved
grants on our website, we also take the time to personally contact each applicant to deliver the news. It's often a joyous moment.

While there is an emotional element to confirming our decision to
grant, it is also essential to communicate the terms of the grant in writing. Clarity around the grant's purpose, the terms of the funding, and the
expectations we have for the partnership are essential.

At times the grant proceeds just as envisioned by the charity. Their goals are realistic and they have a well-thought-out plan for implementation. The funding from the partner is all that is required to ensure the project hums. At other times either staff or the grantmaking committee will suggest ways to improve the donor's participation and the ultimate success of the proposed project.

One particular project comes to mind. A small, growing organization approached us to provide significant core funding to ensure their program could be delivered effectively over a three-year period. Saying yes to their proposed funding timetable would have, in our opinion, been detrimental to the organization's ongoing viability at the end of our grant cycle. At the end of three years, their plan would continue to have the same reliance on our large grant without having built in a plan to continue attracting a broader base of core committed donors. This felt like a trap for them and for us.

To ensure we would encourage both a broadening of support and an exit strategy for us, we structured the grant to stimulate the expansion of their donor base. A large investment was made in the partner in year one. In subsequent years, our funding was tied to their success at attracting new donors. New donor dollars that flowed into the organization in year two would be matched by our foundation. In year three, two new donor dollars would need to be raised to attract our investment. As well, we modified the maximum amounts we were offering to limit our investment on a declining basis over the three years. This would ensure that when our participation ended in the fourth year, there would be a new, motivated core group of donors who would take over the vacuum created by our departure. This type of strategic thinking allowed an empowered fundraising department to raise funds over the course of our grant, leveraging the power of our partnership with others.

Conditional grants are another way to ensure a successful relationship. In some cases, we perceive an area that needs to be addressed prior to proceeding with a financial partnership. When the issue is resolved, it allows for our grant to proceed. One organization approached us for major funding for a large educational facility that would serve a major metropolitan area. However, initial donors to the campaign were drawn from cities removed from the organization's geographic location. How could we stimulate greater giving by those who actually resided and worked in the same city? In that particular case, we offered a conditional grant that would trigger funding only when a certain threshold of major donor funding was pledged from donors residing in the city where the school was located. Fortunately, this occurred, allowing for broader local ownership by others for the initiative.

Another option for granting is to create a challenge for the organization to overcome before funding flows. This is a strategic role for a grantmaker: unless the major donor takes a stand on situations, the charity is not forced to change. On one occasion, we saw value in the events an organization was delivering as a part of its core programming. However, the cost of delivering the events was clearly being subsidized by free money coming from donations, even though beneficiaries were able to pay for services received. In the case of this organization, we challenged them to demonstrate that the cost of holding their events could be covered by earned revenue. If they were successful at achieving this goal in a year, our funds would flow to their new initiative. Orienting grants to create longer-term sustainability is frequently a focus of matching, challenge, and conditional granting.

Before creating a matching, challenge, or conditional grant, it is important to dialogue with the charity to ensure that such a plan is reasonable and achievable by them. Frequently, they will be delighted to be given a tool that expands their fundraising ability, as other donors are attracted to giving when their donation is multiplied by others. Creativity and an insight into charity operations both allow for a well-leveraged grant. But too much creativity, when not done in consultation with the partner, can create burdensome strings attached to the funding that detract the organization from its clear goals. Wisdom in applying a leveraged opportunity is necessary.

Conversations for your pilgrimage

1. How do you communicate your grant decisions?
2. Have you made grants that are conditional or have a challenge or matching aspect? What have been the results of such grants?

13

Creative responses

Güemes (Day 12)

In the mornings there wasn't much to do in the shared semi-darkness except to quietly stuff my toiletry bag in my backpack, fill my water bottle, and launch out wordlessly. Some albergues provide a breakfast of sorts—this one just scattered a few store-bought mini-muffins on the table beside instant coffee and hot chocolate. Jaffer and I gave it a pass, betting we would soon find an open coffee shop on this Sunday morning.

Walking past a grim prison, we were astonished at an imposing rock formation at the end of the beach—and soon saw that our path wound up it. The trail was made of sand, with rock jutting out at various stages. It took considerable effort to climb higher and higher to follow the winding, broken trail. The view from the peak, however, was breathtaking in the early morning haze.

Upon descent, a five-kilometer walk along yet another beach awaited. We followed a French couple who removed their boots and meandered in the churning water. We kept our boots on and stayed on the harder, wet sand, eventually passing them by. Noja was the town at the end of the beach, so upon arrival we stopped for coffees and then launched inland. Our trail now took us through villages, past little churches, amid grazing cattle and sheep, until finally, at the limit of our capability, we arrived in the village of Güemes.

The various camino guidebooks were unanimous in praise of the private albergue in Güemes. Its owner is a retired priest, and his family's property, owned by their private foundation, had been converted into a generous rest

stop for the weary. All proceeds were by donation only, and served to reim-
burse the albergue for expenses of meals, lodging, and hospitality. On arrival,
volunteers handed us a cup of cold water. They beckoned us in for a late,
complimentary lunch. They showed us to our rooms (well-built, roomy cabins
with solid bunk beds), and invited us to their evening communal meal eaten
in the open air at a long table on the patio. They created a great sense of
community and solidarity, which we needed if we were going to keep pressing
onward.

This was a living example of philanthropy in action. What a place of
renewal and grace!

Over the course of the due diligence process, the reviewer will often become attached to an organization's personnel and their mission, and may
believe the project should be funded. Alternatively, evidence might arise
during the process that clearly indicates a partnership is not to be recommended. The grantmaking committee, however, occasionally arrives at a
different conclusion than the reviewer, for various reasons. Whatever the
result, the rationale for the declination should be clearly communicated to
the applicant.

At times, we develop perceptions about an organization and its leadership that impact whether or not a project will be funded. Rightly or wrongly,
the intangible nature of the chemistry between the two parties is a reality
and should not be discarded when determining whether a funder moves
ahead with the grant. Some people are just not meant to work together.

In most cases, one recognizes this early on in the process, and a full
application from the organization is not encouraged. But in some cases,
the lack of congruence between the personalities of the two organizations
becomes apparent only after the due diligence process is well underway.

This is the most difficult news to communicate to a potential applicant
as there may not be anything overtly wrong with their organization—however, the style of its approach or the content of their activities is not valued

by the giver. In some cases, where we sense a disconnect, we make the decision to give a small grant and walk with the organization through the term of the relationship, open to having our attitudes changed. In others, we communicate our declination in writing regretfully yet honestly.

Following our grantmaking meeting, we offer feedback to any applications that were declined at the meeting. This is challenging, but it is also our duty. First of all, just about everyone we meet in the charitable sector is a great person. They have given their heart, soul, sweat, and tears into their calling, and they wouldn't be there if they didn't believe in it. We owe it to them to communicate the truth.

We recognize that declinations are made by a fallible committee. In the past, we've made some decisions that we regret. But the reality is also that many grant applications we receive are not top quality. Many projects are hurriedly conceived, poorly designed, not aligned to the organizational mission, or ask for unreasonable amounts of money. The most common pitfall I find is that applicants are excessively optimistic about how long it will take to achieve the goals stated in the application.

Investing time into communicating even unwelcome news is highly valued by organizations. Frequently we hear that many major donors approached for funding neglect to communicate their decision back to the charity. Some do not even respond to a letter of inquiry, leaving the organization bewildered and uncertain.

Smaller family foundations tend to lack staffing and aren't equipped for responding to the volume of inquiries coming their way. In most of these cases, family members volunteer their own time, and often have existing linkages to charities with whom they have great affection, interest in funding and in being involved. Adding more relationships on top of the ones we are already managing may not be desired. Yet even if this is the case, foundations should still accept the responsibility of communicating that status. A simple system can be created that communicates concisely, closing the loop on the relationship with a potential grantseeker and providing feedback in a timely fashion. Alternatively, you can outsource this to organizations like Stronger Philanthropy.

Consideration needs to be given about the longevity of the partnership with charities. In some instances—especially early on in the relationship with a new partner—a short-term commitment is a good place to begin. This allows for assessment of the value of the partnership within defined parameters and without unduly raising expectations. Later, when the grantmaker is convinced a longer-term relationship is in order, a lengthier partnership may evolve.

We state the length of the term at the front end of any granting relationship. This allows for clear planning by the charity for future sustainability, and gives the grantmaker freedom from the expectations of ongoing donations to the charity. We typically have about a 20 percent turnover each year in terms of the number of new charities with which we enter into a funding relationship. This means some of the older charities with which we've partnered for several years drop off for a period. But they expect that because we communicate it. It's important to keep your funding dynamic to motivate fresh, creative action, and not become stagnant with predictable funding to the same charities year after year.

Of course, charities want larger and multi-year partnerships. This is also often desirable for the donor as well, as it offers an opportunity to journey together with an organization over a longer term where a longer-term creative endeavor is underway. Impact is difficult to assess after a short period of time. As a partnership evolves, a willingness to commit to a multi-year relationship can naturally occur. Donors will benefit by narrowing the number of organizations they partner with and by diving deep into the joys of a sustained relationship.

Saying yes today will also one day mean saying no. Both grants and the commitment of a major donor to a project or an organization's purpose will one day reach their limits. The beauty of being clear about the terms of a grant at the outset of a relationship is that it allows for a natural and healthy end of the grant.

When organizations receive multi-year partnerships from us, we communicate at the beginning of the relationship that the commitment to the grant will one day end. This is a prudent and healthy arrangement. At the front end of a grant, the organization is aware that, within a defined period of time, they will need to look elsewhere for ongoing funding. Our particular policy states that a year's hiatus from granting will follow a large, multi-year granting relationship. This ensures the grant ends with dignity for the organization as well as for the donor, with the relationship intact. Indeed, the conclusion of a successful grant is worth celebrating together.

One memorable evening, several of us gathered at the Hard Rock Café in the market district of Ottawa at the conclusion of Street Level—an occasional gathering of Canada's inner-city outreach workers at a national conference which we supported for a few seasons. These frontline warriors face the daily reality of poverty, death, addiction, and abuse among those they walk alongside as friends. Street Level brings them together to weep for the pain, to manage the trauma, to learn together, and to celebrate the small successes of people who live on the margins of social acceptability. A garage band called Outrider, led by conference chair Tim Huff, strutted its stuff, playing Rolling Stones cover tunes in a raucous ending to the event. The bar was packed with conference delegates shouting and dancing in unison to *You Can't Always Get What You Want*. Much like many of the Psalms, it's an appropriate hymn of emotional angst and realism by those who bear witness to the worst of the human condition.

Too often, we don't tend to celebrate charitable activity. But these folks taught me that we need to gather to honor what has been accomplished, remember what has been lost, grieve for the broken world we inhabit, and reignite passion to keep moving forward. We live in this middle place, a time of now and not yet, where we celebrate small miracles and in the same breath, lament for the work that is yet to be done. As donors to great causes, stirring successes, and disappointing failures, are we dancing and shouting together?

Conversations for your pilgrimage

1. How do you communicate a positive or a negative response to a grant application? Do you offer reasons for your decision? Why or why not?

2. Are your grant recipients aware of how long their funding with you will last? Do you have an exit strategy? Have you communicated it?

14

Evaluating progress

Boo de Piélagos (Day 13)

I woke early enough to take a photo of the sunrise, and with that spectacular view filling my soul, spontaneously decided to begin the day on my own. I wrote a note to the still-sleeping Jaffer saying that I would meet him a few hours down the road at the café beside the cathedral in the city of Santander. Though I'd never been there, it would be a fail-safe meeting place. The camino always passed by each city's main downtown church; there had to be a café beside the cathedral.

Walking solo, I drank in those early morning hours when the birds were still chirping, and descended eleven kilometers from my rural retreat to a flat bike path that took me straight into the town of Somo. Like many of the towns on the Camino del Norte, it was a beach town, but it also offered ferry service across a large bay to the capital of Cantabria province, the sizable city of Santander.

The ferry was little more than a wooden boat with tires nailed to its sides to cushion rapid-fire landings at the docks. Despite the rustic transport, it was an enjoyable thirty-minute commute from small town to big city, and I drank in the sea air and the feeling of floating across the harbor.

I found the cathedral ten minutes after arrival, and immediately ordered a breakfast of churros y chocolate and relaxed in the sun. Jaffer arrived sooner than I expected, so he ordered his coffee and rested, while I took the liberty of walking over to the church for a look.

Just casually popping into churches along the camino can become a jarring reminder of the cost of our faith. On display was the relic of a fourth-century saint, Celedonius: the remains of the martyr's brain were encased in a silver mold of his head. He had been beheaded by the Romans, and was adopted as the patron saint of Santander. Here he was before me; what would he say if he could still speak?

We began walking out of the city down an impressive, tree-lined promenade. We were an odd sight to urban Spaniards going about their daily routines—we were out of place with our hiking clothes, backpacks, hats, and walking sticks. But even in the city, there were occasional residents who wished us a "buen camino."

We continued for twenty-one more kilometers in the intense heat of a Spanish noon. By mid-afternoon, we were once again depleted as we arrived at our destination, Casa Piedad, a private albergue—the place was spotless and welcoming. Without delay, Piedad, the owner, volunteered to launder our sweaty clothes, urged us to shower, and even offered huge, thick cotton towels—such a luxury after weeks of using the minuscule, quick-drying chamois cloth favored by hikers. I was grateful for these small mercies and for her unexpected generosity. With the desperate exhaustion we were feeling, these small acts of kindness gave us life.

ALBERGUE
PIEDAD

BOO DE PIÉLAGOS
680 62 00 73

A dilemma for grantmakers and charities alike is measuring success of activity when impact takes years to achieve. It is a challenging—and even audacious—exercise to link grant dollars to the social and cultural change that we expect through our grantmaking. A generation of grantmakers has attempted to demonstrate return on investment with minimal success.

Part of the problem is that grantmakers fund activities that generate outputs; we rarely think in terms of the ultimate impact we would like to see. We invest in tangible projects that require an outlay of funds to accomplish a purpose—building a classroom, hiring a staff person, supplying materials, or producing a video. These are relatively easy to measure, and charities have become increasingly responsible at reporting these metrics back to donors. But surely we long for more than this in our philanthropy. More than outputs, we long for enduring impact.

Philanthropy includes lofty illusions of changing the world, raising up a generation, educating the young, or defeating poverty. Only by walking alongside an issue or a charity over the long term will we begin to see movement and an eventual impact from persistent investment.

Another issue is that evaluation has typically been the task of an outsider: we want an independent, objective assessment of an organization's success at achieving predetermined goals. As funders we attempt this, or we hire third parties to evaluate. However, outsiders are not generally aware of the complex fabric that knits together nonprofit achievements: the relationships, motivations, diverse players, and complicated context. Impact by charities is much harder to measure than the bottom line of businesses.

To evaluate, we sit in judgment on activity and results. We unconsciously deliver the message: fail to meet your goals, and funding will be cut. This leads to donor-mandated accountability with fear as a driver, rather than encouraging an internally generated hunger for learning or a passion by the organization to achieve its own missional impact. A summative evaluation rationalizes results as linear causes and effects which we imagine are determined mechanistically. However, in the soft world of cultural, social, and spiritual change, change and impact cannot be so easily measured.

Michael Quinn Patton, the former president of the American Evaluation Association, proposes a new approach to evaluation that fits well with the grantmakers who seek a more holistic approach. He advocates for "developmental evaluation," a constantly evolving culture of organizational learning that is inherently a part of the charity's culture.[1] This approach is based on trust in the stakeholders of a nonprofit to collectively discover their own way to achieve their mission effectively, and assumes they are motivated by internal drivers.

Evaluation should not fall solely to the funder, but ought to be a core competency of the nonprofit organization, which leads itself in being a community of learning and growth even while the project itself is in

1. See, for example, Quinn Patton's work described here: http://tamarackcommunity.ca/g3s61_VC_2010g.html.

process. Questions charities can be asking themselves include: are we living out our mission in an authentic and meaningful way? What new opportunities are emerging as we undertake our work? How can we learn through past experiences and apply them to our current reality?

A good example of our own journey of understanding evaluation is a long-term partnership we've had with *Context with Lorna Dueck*. This Canadian current affairs program probes spiritual values that are frequently ignored by mainstream media, to explore the stories of faith that undergird many headlines. When we began our relationship with its executive producer, Lorna Dueck, we assisted in helping her launch the process of creating a charitable organization—Media Voice Generation—which would focus on exploring spirituality in Canadian culture through media. We would also be the charitable fundraising arm to empower her media work. Because we trust Lorna, we have evolved with her in understanding how our philanthropy has been successful.

Early projects with her fledgling organization were concerned with measuring numbers of viewers, advertising and donation revenue, mentions in the mainstream media, responses from viewers, and the like. All of these attempts at measurement are helpful, both for internal discipline and awareness of the success of one's product as well as for the donor's assessment of the value it is creating—but they are not enough. Lorna herself would concur that that wasn't the real reason they were doing this groundbreaking work.

Both the donor and the charity were co-investors in this project: not only to create provocative and successful programming, but to soften hearts to a reality beyond the material, and to open eyes to an awareness of the spiritual within the fabric of our daily lives. We soon realized that reporting back statistically would only provide a slice of the impact that was being generated through the programming.

Our approach evolved by exploring with the organization a more anecdotal understanding of whether they were achieving their mandate. What feedback were they receiving from viewers? What platforms for expressing their mission were being used? Was the spiritual expression being advanced merely concerned with people converting to their way of thinking, or were respectful conversations about the spiritual being generated through the show and their online forums?

We weren't looking for people to convert to our way of thinking, or to tally conversions as many organizations used to do. Instead, we wanted to work towards creating a culture where faith could be considered along with the rest of our society's competing claims. Taking a step back from reductionism in measuring statistics and viewing activities as leading to a more holistic spirituality were important steps in evolution for us and for them as we evaluated and journeyed together.

As we continue on this pathway of responsible stewardship, the question that is utmost in our minds as givers is: how can we be assured that these funds will be efficiently and effectively used to achieve our desired impact? What is the SSROI—the Spiritual and Social Return on Investment?

We encourage our grant recipients to define their goals, measure their results, and report back to us on a timely basis and in writing. How can we tell we are doing a good job in our philanthropy unless we are able to assess the outcomes and benefits of the work our partners do? We ask them to set their own goals, and then report back on their rate of success. We also have a system for scoring reports, which then gives us a chance to define how well we are doing at stewardship.

Many charities balk at results-based management—some feel it is unspiritual, others just don't want to go to the effort, while still others are stymied by reducing holistic ministry into a chart. There is easier money elsewhere. That is fine with us. We want to partner with organizations that are willing to examine their actions and adapt them in a constant quest for improvement.

Sometimes we have had to end relationships with organizations that have failed to meet the ability to report back well. When this happens, we attempt to explain clearly why we made our decision, trusting that our honesty will be ultimately helpful to them.

Conversations for your pilgrimage

1. How do you evaluate the progress your grants are achieving? How is success defined?

2. Do charities report back to you in writing?

Strategy

Forjarán mi destino
las piedras del camino.

The stones along the way
Will forge my destiny.

–Nino Bravo[2]

---

2. Bravo, "Un Beso y una Flor," 1972. Translation by author.

15

Building charity capacity

The days are beginning to bleed together with repetitive familiarity. And yet each one holds unique moments. Today, for example, our route took us across the street to the local commuter train station. We hopped on for a two-minute ride over a bridge across a river. To walk this section would have meant a ten-kilometer detour to reach a different pedestrian bridge. Other more daring pilgrims just walk across the railroad trestles to the path on the opposite bank. Avoiding both the lengthy detour and a risky shortcut, we decided to be prudent, not purist, in our quest to walk all the way to Santiago.

As we advanced along the route, we still seemed to be exiting the urban periphery of Santander. After a couple of hours, we reached Requejada for a second breakfast of croissants, coffee, and fresh orange juice. Before we had taken two sips, unexpected and violent cracks of lightning pierced the sky, followed by intense bangs of thunder. Rain poured down, creating heavy reservoirs of water in the tarp roof over the café. We waited out the storm and drained water from the tarp to prevent it from collapsing in on itself.

Thankfully within the hour, the rain had abated, and we continued our walk in a light drizzle. I was an embarrassing spectacle of a man in a poncho wearing shorts, bare legs poking through and backpack protruding behind. The camino *continues to be a humbling experience.*

We finally deviated from busy city traffic, and onto tertiary roads in the hills. We walked up and down through villages and countryside, and as the drizzle ended, made it to Santillana del Mar.

Strategy

Approaching this town was nothing spectacular—a disappointment at first, since we were told it was a favored tourist destination in Spain and we had had higher expectations. But as we entered the town we realized how wrong our first impressions had been. The road dipped below our horizon, and after a few twists and turns, we gradually ascended into a medieval village with ancient stone walls and cobblestone streets embracing us. A well-preserved jewel from twelfth-century Spain was enveloped and hidden by these hills.

When we initially began our philanthropy pilgrimage, we focused on a charity's mission, and whether we had interest in supporting it or not. Organizations we liked got our money. Usually charities would approach us for funding specific projects—large initiatives that helped them continue their mission.

Quickly, though, we discerned that such funding tended not to be strategic. In many cases, these initiatives went on year after year, and it was part of the organization's ongoing outreach. We would happen to give one year, but the next year another donor would be required to donate to this core programming. I grew to view these types of donations as Band-Aids which just covered over a wound for a short time, but didn't address longer-term issues within the organization.

Many large donors have developed the strategic acumen to see beyond giving merely for ongoing programming. An organization's programs are typically funded by stalwart supporters of an organization, yet to fund core programming with major gifts is to lose an opportunity for more meaningful engagement as major donors. Core programming is best left to consistent, smaller donors who hopefully represent the vast majority of an organization's donated revenue. Major gifts can be strategically deployed to leverage new outreach and to provoke change inside and outside the organization.

One way to make a difference is to help strengthen the organization's ability to carry on its mission more effectively. This type of funding, often called capacity building, is not typically seen as a visible need by most donors to charity, but its importance is fundamental to mission fulfillment and to healthy charities. Capacity building honestly assesses the current realities facing organizations, and develops ways to improve performance. When you build capacity you allow an organization to work smarter so they can deliver their programs better.

I latched onto the value of capacity building because of my own personal experience. Prior to my work in philanthropy, I had been an employee of three different charities. For over a decade in my late twenties and early thirties, I focused on spiritual care and leadership development in the developing world. In Colombia I held retreats and workshops with pastors and church leaders to assist them to be better leaders and to supplement their meager theological education. Later, using my fluency in Spanish, I worked for an American charity as a trainer for Hispanics in the US and with Latinos further south. Finally, I relocated to the Philippines and later back to Canada to provide staff training and care for a third organization whose employees worked in Asia.

While these were three very different charities, they were united by a common experience. Staff were motivated and passionate in their work, but their dedication to the mission, rather than pay, was the motivator. Needless to say, these were organizations that lacked funds, and our common experience was that we all lacked the tools to do our work well. Charities had a hard enough time raising funds for their programming, but creating healthy environments for charity life was sorely lacking. The result was that staff often suffered—morale was low, people burned out, and all staff were less than effective as a result.

Donating towards projects that are considered overhead is not immediately appealing to the general public. We are accustomed to understand charity involvement as donations that immediately impact beneficiaries—the child with a bloated belly living in a thatched roof hut, the homeless woman pushing a rusty shopping cart, and the stubble-faced man, eyes crazy from mental illness—these icons that populate our imaginations and inspire emotional pocket-emptying. But we forget that these same organizations rely on donation revenue to pay for heat and hydro, software and new phones, fundraisers, graphic artists, and receptionists.

On one hand we complain that charities are not run professionally or competently, by well-qualified individuals equipped with the latest technologies. On the other hand, we grouse when we see administration and fundraising costs inch up year after year. The public often squeezes charities into a catch-22 with no way out for charity leaders who want to create healthy and effective vehicles for delivering services. Charities with low overhead are likely not on the cutting edge of keeping up with industry standards, or somehow are masking their true overhead costs by burying them in program costs. Yes, there are those with exceedingly high overhead costs which must be held accountable—but these are exceedingly rare. Funders must move away from this facile and naïve approach of measuring charity effectiveness.

During my years with our foundation, I developed a strategy that would grant funds to charities for capacity building as a portion of our giving portfolio. This mechanism would address issues of organizational health, and offer grants to improve the ongoing sustainability and success of charitable work.

This has led us to grant in areas not typically emphasized in grant applications. With this capacity building focus, we did not sponsor charitable programming; instead, we tackled areas that most donors would not be interested in supporting. The result was that grants were invested into charities for a wide variety of initiatives such as information technology upgrades, professional development of senior leaders, the hiring of additional fundraisers or administrative staffing, and bricks-and-mortar expansion of facilities.

A study published by the Center on Philanthropy at Indiana University reviewed the willingness of foundations to fund the administrative costs of their partners. It revealed the challenges of investing into strengthening the capacity of charities:

> The study found that nonprofits, especially smaller ones, with restricted funding struggle with inadequate administrative and fundraising infrastructure. Inadequate infrastructure compromises organizational effectiveness. Common assumptions are that nonprofits do not spend additional money on overhead because

foundation grant dollars restrict funding to only program costs or nonprofits who report higher administrative expenses do not receive future funding from foundations.[1]

If capacity is built into a charity, greater charity effectiveness can result. This can manifest itself in many diverse ways. With one grant, we invested $150,000 per year over three years to help a large charity's development department expand its reach through hiring more experienced behind-the-scenes personnel. It was astonishing to see growth from $1 million in major donor revenues to $2.5 million in one year, and from twenty-one to seventy-three major donors in the same period. This was directly attributable to the department's enhanced ability to serve donors—in this case, administrative back-end staff to support and supplement the work of an engaging and dedicated vice president of development. With the right support staff, he took off and the entire team became extremely successful.

A different example of building capacity involved a national women's organization. We attempted to help them build their capacity through our challenge to raise earned income through conference fees. For years their conferences had been unsustainable and were propped up by outside donors, but our challenge to them was to award a grant of $25,000 on the condition that their next year's audited statements demonstrated a surplus from their conferences. With this challenge, they were successful in reviewing their operations and creating a measure of ongoing sustainability for their programming. A challenge like this pushed the organization to take seriously their own latent potential for earned revenue and to act on it.

A third example involved helping a relief-and-development organization build capacity through covering the costs associated with training staff. The leadership team received workshops and a retreat over the course of the year which allowed them to solidify their strategic approach as an organization and to build a sense of camaraderie. With this combination of increased knowledge and experiential learning, staff were empowered to do their jobs more effectively. As well, the notion of team was built among management, and these relationships impacted the quality of work done by the organization as trust had been built.

Eventually I realized that the greatest need for capacity building was with smaller, less developed organizations. Yet many of these were too small to qualify for our grants, and working with so many exceeded our own capabilities. Clayton Rowe, national program director for World Vision's

1. Rooney and Frederick, "Overhead," 3.

Canadian programs, attended one of our capacity building workshops, and became inspired. He presented me with a unique plan. World Vision would require start-up funding for a capacity-building emphasis with small charities already doing work with children-at-risk in Canadian urban centers. Our seed capital would launch this initiative that would then deliver training modules on charity capacity building for representatives of these organization. Called FreeForm, this new program eventually benefited dozens of organizations for a decade. With one strategic, multi-year grant, we solidified the organizational development for many charities through the wealth of accumulated experience of Canada's largest and most successful charity. I see this grant as being one of our most strategic uses of money over the years.

What we look for in our capacity-building projects is to answer the question: How will this organization be made more effective through the application of these funds? As well, we've frequently followed a strategy that challenges charities to come up with a portion of the funding which we then match. This allows for ownership by the charity in activity that will directly benefit their internal operations. We have found organizations to be deeply grateful for this emphasis on funding a defined project that is typically part of an organization's overhead expenses.

Conversations for your pilgrimage

1. What kind of investment could you make into the capacity of charities?
2. If charities exist for social betterment, does it really matter whether our donations are destined towards overhead?

16

Examples of capacity building

Comillas (Day 15)

We had stayed overnight in an albergue *that both Jaffer and I agreed was rather creepy—it felt like the owners might have inherited an inn from their parents, and hadn't had the motivation to change anything since they had died a generation before. Medieval knickknacks crowded every available space, including figures of Jesus and plaster replicas of saints, random empty bottles of mysterious liqueurs, plates decorated with places visited, unread books piled high. The place needed a thorough dusting and more than a makeover.*

Walking outside became a rude wake-up call at seven in the morning. The day promised to be one of constant rain. And this wasn't just a misty drizzle, it was pouring. So we walked wet.

The idea of walking in the rain is one we generally avoid: we drive in our warm cars, we find shelter, and, at the very minimum, we use an umbrella. But once you surrender to the idea that you're going to get wet, walking in the pouring rain is not such a bad thing. It was ten degrees cooler than the hot days we'd experienced. I trundled along with my poncho blowing in the wind, and feeling a band of moisture snaking across my back where my backpack came in contact with my body.

Around ten we stopped in a town for our second breakfast—hot coffee was a priority to warm us up. After a good rest, Jaffer and I continued, but on exiting the town, we walked by an open church. Most of the churches we passed on the camino *were closed in the mornings when we happened to walk by, but this one had its doors flung open. I encouraged Jaffer to continue forward, and that I would catch up to him later.*

It turned out the church was part of a Cistercian monastery, and they made and sold their own cheeses. I chatted with a monk and ended up buying a quarter round of cheese. He wanted to sell me more, but I was cognizant that I would end up carrying the weight.

By this point the rain had intensified, and Jaffer was nowhere in sight. I knew we had Comillas as our destination, so I just set out for that town, which was seven kilometers distant. Because of the rain, I decided to take the highway route—a bit shorter than the meandering pathway—but it made for an especially damp walk with passing trucks and cars splashing even more moisture my way. As I walked, I reflected, and felt myself moving inward with the rhythmic pounding of my staff against the pavement. Walking with Jaffer had been meaningful and we had enjoyed each other's company, but I sensed I needed more time alone. I realized it was time for me to say goodbye to my friend.

I stumbled upon Jaffer at a hotel café in Comillas and we ordered coffees and sandwiches and tried to dry out. I took a deep breath; then told him I was reaching a moment where I needed to embrace the solitude of the camino. He said he also was feeling the need to walk alone. I deeply appreciated my time with this non-judgmental, wise man who quoted Rumi over lunches, and who loved the expansive possibilities of silence. Awkwardly and abruptly, we said adios, *not knowing if we would ever see each other again. Jaffer continued on to the next town, and I found lodging in Comillas.*

Walking with Jaffer day by day built my capacity as well as his. We needed the support of each other to motivate and encourage us in our long walk. But the goal of capacity building is to stand on your own feet, and it was time to walk alone.

Building one charity's capacity looks different from building another's. Often it does not require an expensive solution, though it will inevitably involve an intentional outlay of expenses. Other options require considerable planning and expense.

Here are some possibilities for what capacity building can look like:

1. *Information technology:* Leveraging the power of the Internet and computer technology is a great place to begin for philanthropists who are ready to build charity capacity. IT solutions to help organizations expand their presence can range from simple to complex, from free to expensive. Organizations can discover their online voice with social media strategies using free or inexpensive marketing tools such as blogs, podcasts, Twitter, Facebook, Flickr, and YouTube, or MailChimp e-newsletters. Online platforms for managing a donor database are also available for small monthly amounts. A student intern could be hired to take leadership of the organization's digital presence.

   At the other end are more expensive options to enhance effectiveness. Developing integrated websites is often a painstaking process that usually proves productive and builds community in the long run. Other solutions could include updating needed software or hardware, acquiring smartphones for key staff, or developing an online store. I remember the joy and relief at UrbanPromise Toronto when a grant to provide staff with new laptops was announced. Until then they had been working on ten-year-old clunkers that sapped effectiveness from their outreach.

   IT is an aspect of organizational development that has the potential to be expensive, so a donor needs to exercise caution. Charities often don't have the internal expertise to evaluate whether technology solutions are either reasonable in cost or the best technological approach to pursue—and information technology developers have their own interests at stake as they sell their services. Likewise, most grantmakers lack the expertise to evaluate these solutions. I fear at times we have funded expensive IT solutions that were Cadillacs when a Ford would have been sufficient. We are slowly learning to rely on third-party experts to offer their wisdom as we evaluate proposed solutions.

2. *Support staffing:* Where would any of our organizations be without the valuable support of those who administer, fundraise, and communicate? An executive director who finds himself licking stamps and printing labels for mailings may need to hire an administrative assistant or an intern so he can be more fully deployed into a strategic leadership role. Larger organizations may have matured to the stage of

needing qualified fundraisers or grant-writers. Perhaps there is a need for a dedicated social media coordinator to increase web traffic. Creating meaningful platforms for volunteers to offer their capabilities is also important for any size of charity; a paid volunteer mobilizer may be a desired staff position.

No one wants to invest in bloated administrative costs so funding for staffing is an important type of grant to link the investment to an increase in outreach. In one of our grants, we participated in funding the hiring of an additional staff person at a small inner-city storefront outreach, in order to allow the overworked executive director more time to focus on strategic leadership and fundraising. But we made this investment with an eye to seeking growth in annual income and tangible products (such as a written strategic plan), and ultimately an increase in numbers of youth served through this expanding organization.

3. *Fundraising solutions:* Philanthropists can assist an organization in multiplying its potential through the development of new fundraising strategies. Many charities use annual banquets or golf tournaments–but organizations need to dispassionately assess whether the outlay of funds, time, and effort is worth the net benefit. More creative and productive fundraising is now happening through inviting potential donors to view their work in the developing world, launching a cycleathon, climbing the CN Tower, and in the case of prostate cancer, growing mustaches. Having a large donor underwrite the initial outlay of expenses is one way to trumpet a net benefit to the organization.

Back-end support of one-time fundraising events is one way to build capacity; another is through investing in hiring fundraising staff. This type of capacity building has curb appeal for donors interested in visibly leveraging their financial investment—it's easy to measure financial growth—but funders can't expect instant miracles. Donors must be patient in seeing results that are built on relationships, something that is frequently slower to cultivate than we might expect. One rule of thumb suggests fundraisers should cover costs after year one, then expand by a multiple of two and three in each of the succeeding years. However, this does depend on the brand awareness of the organization. Newer organizations may take considerably more time to raise a base of committed donors.

Care must be taken when hiring fundraisers from other organizations—the "donor relationship" belongs to the previous organization, not to the fundraiser, and it would be unethical to expect a fundraiser's contacts to come with her unless at the specific invitation of the donor. A year-long non-compete restriction is appropriate before a professional fundraiser is released to contact people with whom relationships were made while employed by other charities in the past.

4. *Strategic planning:* It may be that new economic realities require an organization to revamp its agenda, or perhaps it has been several years since a strategic visioning process has informed the board and senior management. Philanthropists can invest in an organization becoming stronger and more freshly motivated through the sharpening focus of a planning exercise.

Donors with expertise in this area may find unique fulfillment from offering to lead the organization through this process on a pro bono basis, or at reduced cost. Doing so, however, could lead to an unstated expectation which assumes the donor will fund the organization's future direction. A more detached option would fund hiring an outside professional to lead the process.

Developing a strategic plan when an organization is ripe for change and open to creative, out-of-the-box avenues for mission fulfillment can be a very rewarding experience for donors. Several years back, we partnered with Muskoka Woods Sports Resort to assist them in developing a written strategic vision. Included in this funding was the funding of a retreat for senior leadership, led by an outside expert. All activities were completed and a report of considerable heft was produced but I wondered how our involvement had really helped. A few years later, however, I attended the soft launch of their brand new Leadership Studio—a brilliant expression of innovative thinking that set aside a unique, well-equipped, artistic space for the formation of youth leadership. In his opening remarks, CEO John McAuley credited this explosion of creativity with a fresh vision that had been nurtured years earlier in the womb of the strategic planning retreat we had enabled.

5. *Research:* Paying for a feasibility study or for feedback on existing work is an activity that philanthropists don't often consider when funding charity health. Yet the best-made plans begin with an investment into researching best solutions. Expanding into a new market, developing

a new product, or researching new program offerings all benefit from an expert's technical analysis or from the public's subjective feedback. Costs can vary with feedback being obtained through the use of free or inexpensive web-based surveys like Survey Monkey; alternatively, a professional survey firm could offer the best sort of feedback prior to advancing on expensive and risky projects.

One charity repeated sought our assistance for programming grants year after year, but I had reservations about their mission and whether they were actually doing what they claimed to be doing. To address my concerns, I finally agreed to fund a grant for research, done by a professional firm based in California, which would survey a thousand beneficiaries of the organization's work. I had one caveat for this grant: I wanted to be in the room when the professional firm reported the raw data to the organization. My suspicions were proven correct when the firm, after several months of interviews and number crunching, clearly demonstrated that the organization needed to reconsider its ongoing programming as they were not accomplishing their stated mission and reaching their targeted clientele. This led to a complete organizational overhaul and reconsideration of their operations.

We empowered another kind of research when we were approached by a Briercrest College in Saskatchewan to help them investigate the viability of expanding their offerings to offer streams for First Nations students. They proposed a "slow food" approach: going to the bleak shores of James Bay to listen to and learn from their Cree alumni, gathering First Nations experts to offer counsel in two different forums, and gaining insight in First Nations education from a University of Calgary academic before developing their own solution. Investing in the slow pace of such activity allowed for a more solid, reasonable project—and in this case, greater cultural awareness and buy-in from beneficiaries—going forward.

6. *Consulting*: Consultants get a bad rap because everyone seems to have a story to tell about an unfortunate incident using a consultant. However, an outside set of impartial eyes and ears provides charities with invaluable perspective when attempting to improve organizational performance. Many consultants specialize in specific areas—fundraising, executive search, team dynamics, cultural intelligence, and governance, for example. Philanthropists often have extensive networks

and experience with consultants that would benefit charity leaders, and only require introductions to be made.

7. *Professional development:* An investment into expanding staff capability is a valuable way to encourage charities to reward loyalty and enhance ongoing performance. This can be done through webinars by industry associations such as the Canadian Council of Christian Charities, or through training from other sources such as the Canada Revenue Agency, the Council on Foundations, or the Association of Fundraising Professionals. Organizations can consider investing in obtaining the CFRE (Certified Fund Raising Executive) designation for their fundraisers, something which adds credibility to development staff. They can also explore leadership development opportunities for younger staff with future potential.

In an attempt to proactively seek out granting opportunities in areas that aligned with our foundation's interest in capacity building, we launched a Request for Proposals (RFP) in 2005. The focus of this initiative was the funding of professional development for senior leadership of charities. As part of our capacity building strategy, we wanted to invest in a generation of leaders who were committed to remaining with their organizations for a minimum of two additional years beyond the term of the grant. With successful grant recipients, we agreed to fund half their education needs, with the board of the organization challenged to provide the remaining half from the charity's reserves. It would be an investment into the charity's ongoing health.

This initiative resulted in twenty-one leaders from as many organizations receiving grants towards both formal education (including master and doctoral level degrees) and informal professional development (coaching, seminars, workshops, etc.). It resulted in Jamie McIntosh from International Justice Mission obtaining his master's degree in justice and advocacy from Oxford University, and Aileen van Ginkel from Evangelical Fellowship of Canada obtaining her doctor of ministry from Tyndale Seminary. Both leaders represent the types of solid and committed charity leaders worth investing in—this education bears fruit years into the future for the charities they touch.

Involvement in this sort of capacity building is an impetus for an organization to keep stepping up its game, and signifies an outsider's thoughtful participation in the organization's ultimate, long-term success.

8. *Bricks-and-mortar:* Capacity can be extended through physical means as well. Perhaps the time has come to invest in expanded facilities—classrooms, offices, meeting rooms, or other programming space—or perhaps existing space needs renovation or a makeover. As these are costly solutions, organizations should ensure that they move ahead with a solid plan to ensure future sustainability: a clear plan will outline the path forward and is often preceded by a stakeholders' survey to determine buy-in by the constituency.

   World Vision Canada is our nation's largest charity, but at one time it was headquartered in a bleak, brown brick bunker in the catacombs of Mississauga's suburban industrial unit sprawl. In the early 2000s they embarked on a risky and bold plan to relocate to a major artery with clear access to the 401—the major highway system running past Toronto's Pearson airport. Along with many others, we were approached to consider involvement. The result is a light and airy, professional space, which undoubtedly encourages greater productivity than their former cramped and dark offices. Indeed, they have grown so much in the past decade that they have continued to expand their updated facilities with new additions.

9. *Spiritual care:* One frequently overlooked element for building charity capacity is the area of spiritual care for leaders and staff. We cannot ignore the potential for spiritual care to provide charitable organizations with a stronger, healthier, and more centered environment. From hiring a chaplain to hosting a prayer retreat, the options for addressing the spiritual needs of staff are many.

   Several years ago we worked with Yonge Street Mission, Canada's premier inner-city ministry dedicated to reaching out to the homeless and those gripped by poverty in the city of Toronto. For twenty years, its then-CEO, Rick Tobias, had been laboring on the fringes of urban life where he had led the organization to greater relevance and prominence in the city core. Witnessing the desperate choices and addictions of fellow humans on a daily basis can grind down the soul, and Rick needed renewal. We collaborated to assist in a year's guided sabbatical that involved retreats in monasteries and an overseas trip to gain perspective and renew vision. Following the year's hiatus, he returned refreshed and committed to ten more years of leading the organization with fresh lenses.

10. *Partnership:* A final way to strengthen an organization with limited resources is by teaming up with another to share the back office. One charity opens its doors for another to move in. Others share a book-keeper or a receptionist; others pool computer servers and photocopi-ers. Larger organizations open their doors to their smaller cousins to provide free meeting space or consulting in best practices. Productive partnerships can result if dissimilar organizations cooperate, allowing the strengths of each to be appreciated and savings to accrue to both.

The second floor of a nondescript South Vancouver office building once witnessed this type of cooperation. International China Concern (an organization assisting severely disabled Chinese children) and Ratanak Foundation (a Cambodia-focused outreach) shared space with a pastoral counselor and a local church's offices. Each had their own offices for the small staffs, but the common space was graced with funky, secondhand furniture, throw pillows, and the smell of organic coffee.

When a charity builds its capacity, it does so to improve the bottom line—serving its clients in a more effective fashion. Organizations that are becoming stronger should be ready to demonstrate that their clients will be positively impacted by the internal improvement. While challenging contexts can paralyze us, they also provide an opportunity to tackle need with new approaches and an inspired imagination. Many opportunities exist for philanthropists to come alongside in creative collaboration in making these organizations stronger and more effective.

Conversations for your pilgrimage

1. Do you feel your grants have been like Band-Aids, just covering a problem for a year, and then being reapplied? How could your granting become more strategic?

2. What kinds of capacity building do you see the greatest need for? How could this be used to strengthen your favorite charities?

17

Funding creativity

I walked out of Comillas, now truly alone—and immediately, I chose the wrong road. It was going to be one of those days, and I now no longer could rely on anyone else. I walked for twenty minutes in the early morning sun before gradually realizing my mistake—yellow arrows were not appearing on my path!—so I backtracked and started over. Signage on the Camino del Norte is not always reliable, and you really have to keep your eyes peeled to stay on track.

The day continued uneventfully through woods and villages until the final descent into Unquera, a small riverside town on the Cantabrian side of the border with Asturias. When signage was scarce, I relied on an app on my phone that plotted my location by GPS against the camino routing. The app directed me up a mountain ridge on a paved path, then recommended turning left off the pavement to a dirt pathway marked by wheel ruts from a tractor. Though the app suggested following the wheel marks, I was confronted by a sign: it was a camino waymarker that had been lightly painted over with grey. Again, this wasn't that uncommon an experience as we had found that sometimes farmers would discourage walkers from using their land by paint-ing over signs.

The path quickly led me into a logging operation in a eucalyptus forest. Tracks created by the machinery went everywhere, and it became impossible to follow what had originally been the way. I made a few different attempts, but they all dead-ended. I knew below me at the bottom of the mountain was the road leading to town, so I reasoned going down was my best option. Forging ahead, I descended.

It was a huge mistake I immediately regretted. The mountain slope was steep and within minutes the forest surrounded me, and worse, brambles and thorny vines tangled my legs as I fought through with my staff. There was no pathway forward. The further ahead I struggled, the worse it became. I was sliding downhill and returning back became impossible. My backpack weighed me down, and created extra volume that made it even more difficult to squeeze through the vines. Exhausted, I sat down in the forest for a gulp of water and to assess my options.

The only reasonable choice was to advance through the pain. Thorns pierced my exposed flesh—legs, arms, neck, and face—but I struggled forward, blood and sweat mixing in a trickle down my legs and arms. I feared I was walking away from the road, so I kept adjusting my orientation. I decided to scale a rocky ledge to better view my options, so I placed my staff on top of the rock, and hauled my way up. Once on top, I sat down to catch my breath, my heart beating heavily. I took only a sip of water as I had only a half inch of water left in my bottle and feared running out. Taking another breath, I resolved to move ahead despite the agony. Unaware in this moment of exhaustion, I left the beautiful gift of my staff behind on the rocky ledge.

After two long hours of battling vegetation, a clearing finally emerged. Miraculously, the road was just below me. I found myself perched at the top of a ten-foot wall next to the roadway, so I inched along it until I could throw my backpack down to the asphalt and then hang over the lip to drop to the road.

Two kilometers later, I finally found relief: an open bar where I drank two icy cold Cokes in quick succession. A curious idea came to me as I recovered and reflected on this experience: perhaps my staff had stayed behind in the woods because I no longer had a need of a crutch. With that liberating thought, I smiled and splurged 25 euros on a simple hotel room where I cleaned up, disinfected my scrapes and cuts, and collapsed.

HOTEL CANAL
UNQUERA - CANTABRIA
B-39235866

As we continued on our philanthropy pilgrimage, there was a constant temptation to be a crutch for organizations. This is one of the places where many philanthropists find themselves stuck in the brambles. If an organization has a vibrant, relevant mission, they reason, then why not fund their favorite charity's ongoing programming every year?

Some larger grantmakers choose this option—this may give joy to some and ongoing funding certainly is essential for charities. But this wasn't where we had positioned ourselves. Instead, we saw our grants as an opportunity to inject creative capital into the charity at a particular moment in its history. We were uniquely positioned to jump-start organizations that were launching new endeavors and to help them move beyond where their committed donor base was willing to go. New ideas don't just happen; they need the impetus from somewhere. I'm convinced that major private donors have a unique and unusual potential role in advancing innovative solutions through investment in these sorts of riskier projects.

As a result of this belief, we developed an emphasis on innovation that invests into new, creative approaches to addressing need. While capacity building was one wing of our strategy, investing in innovation became the other wing. The technical nature of capacity building funding is balanced by jump-starting an expansion of charitable programming when it is approached innovatively. Our belief here is that the charity's core donor base can and should fund ongoing program delivery of an organization, allowing for a measure of sustainability. But when a charity seeks expansion to serve a new market or to pilot a creative and untried programming approach, it can rely on larger, strategic donors with a higher appetite for risk.

We look for charitable partners who are ready to move beyond the status quo. These are organizations that have acquired a holy discontent with comfortable normalcy and the same old middle-of-the-road, safe routines. Being in a place of discontent is an opportunity to think creatively, and hopefully, to move to the margins for service.

One spring morning early in my philanthropy career, a thick and well-researched proposal landed on my desk. I was astonished. In these earlier days, I had been receiving all kinds of proposals—from simple handwritten appeal letters requesting whatever we could spare to glossy million-dollar asks sent special delivery. I read them all. But this one was different. This document spoke of heavy investment of time and strategic thoughtfulness in the way the content was presented. It spoke of opening a community center in a neighborhood of my city that had over 60 percent new immigrants. It was seeking core startup funding for the launch of this initiative.

The proposal was to purchase an unused fitness center in an industrial area off the main street, and convert it into the locus of operations for a group of first generation Filipino-Canadians who had learned the hard way what was required for settling into a new country. Gateway Centre for New Canadians aspired to serve all immigrants with ESL classes, computer training, driver education classes, refugee settlement services, career counseling, dance fitness, tae-kwon-do, and more. In particular, their focus centered on immigrant youth.

While they had the limited backing of a denominational group, there were a few red flags. Their charitable status had been applied for, but had not yet been awarded by the federal government so they were still working under a local church's charitable status. The board consisted not of objective outsiders, but of program staff and the executive director. And the proposal was still just a dream—nothing was yet operative.

Normally, an organization at this stage of development would have received a gentle declination, urging them to return when their ducks were in a row. But I found personal alignment in this initiative: the neighborhood where Gateway wanted to open shop was the very one where my local church had contemplated starting our own community center a few years earlier. I knew firsthand that the need existed and continued to go unmet by other local agencies.

The driver behind the program was Julius Tiangson, a fiery Filipino-Canadian accountant/pastor whose business-savvy approach assured us that what he was attempting was worth the risk. We also had a point of contact in that he was from Davao, the same Mindanao city where Karen and I had lived in 1997.

We scuttled our assessment framework, deciding in this case to take a risk on an entrepreneurial immigrant, and investing with them over time. As it was located in our own city, we could remain close to the action and learn through the experience. Karen joined the startup board of the charity once it was awarded its status.

The results have been astounding, though the journey has not been easy for this group. Gateway learned to diversify their funding base, relying not only on individual donors but expanding to larger foundations and even receiving government grants of $2 million for expansion of their services. The little immigrant service that could grew up. It has been extremely satisfying for us to witness Gateway's growth, and to share in this journey.

Strategy

Over Julius's tenure as executive director, Gateway directly served 700 youth with more than 55,000 unique visits per year, coordinated a province-wide settlement program for 1,200 schools and more than 35,000 elementary and high school kids, and created a wide array of twenty-two relevant programs for all ages of immigrants.

Success cannot be measured in statistics alone. In fact, in any philanthropic project, numbers only tell a part of the story. Without the humanity of the story, the skeletal statistics can even be misleading. The story that best displays Gateway's influential impact in the community is one I uncovered on a site visit when we were considering their most recent grant application.

We went through the business of the visit—reviewing growth plans, strategy, current financial status, fundraising results and potential for the future, and project goals and indicators of success. Then Julius took us on a tour of the building, showing us the upgrades and progress since our last visit.

What we didn't expect were the shoes.

Turning a corner, a mountain of shoes and sandals blocked our path. We heard a quiet murmur behind closed doors. Julius whispered an explanation: "It's a Pakistani Muslim group we allow to use our gym on Fridays. More than 200 men and women use this facility for prayers each week."

Just then, a tall, barefoot, bearded figure, clad in white robe and prayer cap, opened the door, and Julius introduced me to a young imam. The imam's first words surprised me. He clasped my hand, looked me straight in the eyes, and gesturing to Julius, said, "This is my brother."

I began to hear story after story that blew apart stereotypes: the Filipino-Canadian evangelical pastor and the Pakistani-Canadian imam who meet together weekly to drink tea, the way the community center has opened its doors in wide-armed generosity to all immigrant groups that had a need, the integration of a misunderstood and maligned group into Canadian society through the resources of their fellow immigrant "brothers and sisters" at the community center. Though the center was a risky endeavor, an incredible, intangible legacy of trust and friendship emerged in addition to the many practical ways hundreds of immigrants were being assisted each week.

Conversations for your pilgrimage

1. Do you grant towards the status quo or are your grants designed to move the charity toward expansion and growth?

2. How much are you willing to risk?

18

Taking risks

After the trauma of the previous day, I slept in and had a late start. Once on the path, however, I immediately entered the Principality of Asturias by crossing the bridge over the river. Spain has seventeen autonomous regions—not all are called provinces or states, and each one seems to have a different set of responsibilities and relationship with the federal state. I thought the Canadian confederation was confusing, but Spain's seemed downright medieval—which, come to think of it, it was! Asturias was the birthplace of the Spanish kingdom, and the center from which the Moors were eventually driven out of the Iberian Peninsula just five centuries ago.

I hiked up the hill away from the river, and as I crested, came face to face with an elderly, wizened gentleman blocking my path. I felt like I had been transported to a fairy tale and was facing a troll in the roadway. He stood on the path next to a small, stone shrine housing a crucifix and weather-beaten statues of saints. Kindly but persuasively, he requested I contribute to light a candle for my camino. Nothing else made sense but to acquiesce, so I gave him a coin and lit a votive. Another prayer for my journey.

After the next town, I continued along the roadway, when suddenly emerging from a parallel path was a pilgrim I recognized from a few stages ago. A tall, elegant Frenchwoman named Catherine stood paralyzed. She relayed to me her confusion—a half-hour earlier she and another pilgrim had exchanged cellphones to input each other's contact information to stay in touch, and she had become distracted. She couldn't find her phone. Her new friend had walked off, she thought, with her cellphone.

We walked together to see if we could catch up. At each café we passed, we asked if they had seen her friend, but no luck. Needing a coffee, and eventually giving up hope, we finally stopped. She was from the city of Orléans and was an architect who worked for the municipality. Her faith was significant to her, and we discussed how one could recover the social space for the sacred in our secular societies. Moments like this were gifts along the camino—sharing information and ideas, and moving forward enriched.

I marched on ahead leaving her to finish her orange juice, and walked the rest of the day alone. The route now began to diverge, multiplying into several parallel, interwoven, alternative paths leading along the Cantabrian coastline. I chose the route away from the water and walking quickly to pass a Scout troop of about twenty Spanish teens walking and singing. Eventually I arrived at a roadside bar which was serving the midday meal. It was now about two in the afternoon, lunch time for the locals, and I was starving.

Normally by this time I would have arrived at my destination and firmed up my lodging for the evening. But due to my late start, I was still en route and my morning croissant had been burned off hours earlier. I decided to stop and enjoy a leisurely two-course meal with the crowning touch of flan for dessert. Then, with energy renewed but with rain once again threatening, I proceeded into the town of Llanes.

My late arrival left me with few options for lodging. The local albergue was full, and I was turned away. It was Friday evening on a summer weekend at the coast, and Spaniards often flock to the beaches on weekends, filling up all hotels and inns. By chance, I ran into an American and a Swedish pilgrim who stood out in the crowds for their backpacks and worried expressions. They were faced with the same dilemma. Together we scoured the Internet and inquired at the tourist office, but all recommendations were to keep walking to the next town, with no assurance of lodging there either. After thirty kilometers of walking today, I just couldn't keep going, nor could they. We pleaded with a local innkeeper who took pity on us, and offered us an unused loft area they kept as an overflow space. As the saying goes, the camino provided.

Strategy

Dr. Joel Orosz, author of *Effective Foundation Management: Fourteen Challenges of Philanthropic Leadership and How to Outfox Them*, believes foundation boards should demand a level of failure in the projects they support. Coupled with this is a learning curve that allows for positive outcomes from even failed projects. Taking significant risks involves funding organizations and projects that fall outside the expected frameworks we establish. Orosz lays down the gauntlet to foundation boards:

> Boards, however, must demand a certain level of experimental failure, for that is the price of doing business in the nonprofit sector, the cost of true innovation, the payment for clearing the kudzu of modest, incremental, "so what?" success. By demanding occasional experimental failure, boards free foundation leaders from their self-imposed, play-it-safe shackles. If not every meal has to be perfect, the French chefs can abandon oatmeal and experiment with exotic new dishes.[1]

Grantmaking that takes us outside our safe places, such as the one we made to the community center for Gateway Centre for New Canadians in the last chapter, can boldly embrace risk. These are the grants which give a grantmaker the greatest satisfaction.

The challenge of innovation is that it is so risky. Yet who more than major donors can afford this kind of risk? Government funding is not typically designated toward riskier initiatives, but to large, stable, blue chip programs. The charity's loyal donor base is already needed for reinforcing ongoing programming. Private foundations and independent major donors are uniquely positioned to take on this risk as they have limited accountability to outside stakeholders. Those who love the potential of charitable innovation need to unashamedly invest in new creative ventures that advance social change. This will likely lead to failures, but through persistent effort and communicating lessons learned through failing, positive change can emerge.

Sean Stannard-Stockton castigates foundations for their tendency to typically play it safe:

> For all their talk about innovation, foundations are in the grip of self-imposed constraints that limit their ability to undertake truly innovative activities. The problem is that most foundation board members believe their primary role is to uphold their fiduciary duty to preserving a foundation's assets and to follow a donor's

---

1. Orosz, *Foundation Management*, 35.

intentions, when in fact their top allegiance should be to the beneficiaries of their foundation's work. It is time for a new interpretation of fiduciary duty that focuses squarely on a foundation's obligation to its beneficiaries.[2]

While many foundations' boards operate conservatively, there is a compelling argument for disbursing grants that innovatively benefit communities, rather than stable decision-making more focused on preserving capital and the longevity of the foundation. Our small foundation was not destined to break new ground in social innovation like industry giants Gates, Buffett, Ford, and Pew. But we still need to be oriented towards taking risks, trying new approaches, and thinking differently.

Two very different grants come to mind when thinking of risks which we have taken in the recent past. Importantly, the purpose of both of these challenging grants is not to impose religion or morality onto the public realm, but to acknowledge and celebrate spiritual heritage, free expression, and the ability to choose one's path openly.

One is the largest grant ever made by Bridgeway Foundation: a seven-figure pledge to Tyndale University College and Seminary to support the expansion of the school to Bayview Avenue, occupying a historic convent run by the Sisters of St. Joseph.

The project itself was noteworthy: we believed it to be the largest fundraising effort ever by a faith-based organization in Canadian history for an aggressive $58-million capital campaign. In a compelling series of circumstances, Brian Stiller, then president of Tyndale, had developed a relationship with the Sisters of St. Joseph who owned a striking convent building full of architectural drama and expansive green areas on one of Toronto's major arteries. It was where former Pope John Paul II had resided during his celebration of World Youth Day several years earlier. Unfortunately, the sisters were aging, and new recruits to the Catholic order were few—downsizing was needed. They were faced with their moment of truth: sell to a real estate developer or keep the property within the faith.

When the evangelical institution came calling, and the Vatican approved the purchase, the stars began to align. Once the two parties agreed on the deal, Stiller began to assess the potential for major donor partners of the school to invest in this new initiative. His bold inquiries led to concerned conversations amongst grantmakers—is this something we can do? Is it too large a project? Who will support it? Are we out of our minds?

2. Stannard-Stockton, "Duty," lines 1–6.

The amounts that Stiller urged all of us to invest in this project were greater than any of us had previously contemplated in a single giving decision. Fortunately, these were amounts we could stretch to give over the long term. But it was the sense of being a community and the trust we had with one another, as well as with Stiller's leadership of the institution, which allowed each potential partner to have the courage to make commitments that would form the groundwork for the campaign.

To be honest, we became severely strained by our bold commitment. The campaign also faced many unforeseen challenges: several senior leadership changes, a crippling economic recession, flatlining enrollment, delays in obtaining city permits, unexpected discoveries when renovating, and a disappointing lack of buy-in from some potential major players. This led to a very slow implementation of the plan. Due to the weakness of the economy in the late 2000s and early 2010s, we maintained our pledge but had to extend our payments to account for losses incurred in our own portfolio. While the grant itself resulted in a successful new campus for the institution, we eventually came to believe that we over-pledged. We ended up extending our payments from seven to twelve years, and our aggressive pledge severely restricted new grants to other charities.

Yet we couldn't foresee the 2008 recession, and such is the nature of risk. Looking back, indicators seemed ripe for success: the growth in private educational options and academic endorsements from the provincial government; an expansion of program offerings such as education and business majors; the beautiful and strategically located facility on a major avenue with a seemingly divinely appointed deal between the Catholics and Evangelicals. Our motive behind this grant was our belief that faith-based educational options within the broad fabric of our diverse Canadian society are essential. This grant, like many others we undertake, propels faith into having greater visibility and presence within our social order. Overall, I think we will agree it was worth the risk.

The other grant that comes to mind as I think of riskier decisions we've made for our grant partners is drastically different in its expression. While in the past we rarely funded startup initiatives (and publicly stated we would not consider these sorts of grants), we have had a long history of involvement with charity entrepreneur Greg Pennoyer, founder of Ottawa's Centre for Cultural Renewal, and editor of the popular and lavishly illustrated Advent guide *God With Us*. Our understanding of his commitment to the role of the arts in championing and opening doors for spiritual expression led us to invest in a startup idea designed to advance a unique idea. His "Incarnation Exhibition," created in partnership with Edmonton curator David Goa, would take a series of artistic masterpieces on the life of Jesus Christ from their European cradles on tour to North America. We contributed some start-up capital to enable the first year of operations for this endeavor.

Such an undertaking, however, was an immense task neither Pennoyer nor Goa was able to foresee, and again, the timing was partly the problem. Once again, the economic climate had constricted donations to innovative, expansive initiatives—charitable donations in the late 2000s were generally channeled to stabilize existing work as donors lacked appetite for participating in the launch of wild-eyed dreams. As well, the vast technical capabilities required to undertake this project were underestimated—it required researchers, writers, art historians, graphic designers, and media specialists, among others. And then there were the complexities of negotiating with museums, insuring the pieces, and raising funds from corporate and mega-donors who desired profile.

Pennoyer is one of the most visionary and tenacious men I know, and he struggled for years to birth this baby. As funding possibilities dried up, he settled on a plan to digitize the exhibition and curate an online site with his vision.[3] It was a far cry from the original vision we contributed toward, but at least we had something tangible to show for his laborious efforts.

While this project was a long and painful struggle in its formation, should it be considered a failure? Well, yes and no. It is true that the initial dream was not accomplished as planned. As we grappled with the slow uptake on this project and witnessed roadblock after roadblock, it produced a conversion of sorts in my thinking. Pennoyer and Goa provoked me and many others to seriously consider the benefit and need for arts and culture funding. We, and many other philanthropists like us, were typically drawn to simpler, more tangible (and seemingly more necessary) projects such as drilling water wells in Africa or stocking up the local food bank. But these two men helped us reorient our own thinking about our responsibility as funders in shaping and contributing to culture. My own perspectives have shifted in the course of our ongoing friendship and I have been permanently changed.

This is a necessary evolution for grantmakers as they grapple with how their funds are ultimately utilized. New grantmakers are attracted to

3. View the online exhibition at http://uencounter.org/.

quick fixes and immediate solutions until they discover there is no such thing, and they've been seduced by the marketing appeal of the competent development director. They usually realize this the third time he knocks on their door.

As donors consider their level of appetite for riskier ventures, they can balance their granting portfolios with what they determine to be a healthy mix of innovative grants along with tried-and-true, blue chip charitable grants. Having a spectrum of such grants in one's portfolio offers grantmakers the ability to continue to reflect, grow, and mature in one's grantmaking over the years.

Conversations for your pilgrimage

1. What grants have you funded that had less-than-rosy outcomes?

2. What did you learn from these experiences? What did your charity partner learn? How did it modify your philanthropy going forward?

19

Examples of innovation

Camargu (Day 18)

I awoke early and departed while my companions slept. As a sunny morning dawned, my walk was solitary and beautiful, weaving in and out along the coastline of imposing bluffs and isolated, sandy beaches between the rocks. At my first real break of the day, I drank orange juice at a café and watched three surfers battle the waves.

As I finished my juice, I slowly began to realize that, because it was the weekend, my lodging problem might continue unless I booked a room. I searched online for available beds but every attempt at each inn, pension, or albergue *for the next hundred kilometers showed as completely booked all weekend long. I made several phone calls, also to no avail. I realized there was nothing else I could do but keep walking; if all else failed, my less-than-preferred fallback plan was to sleep on the beach in Ribadesella. My mantra became "let it go." With every step I walked, I had to let go of all my expectations and know that whatever happened, I would find a place to lay my head tonight—even if that meant the sand of the beach.*

Four kilometers before the Ribadesella beach, I passed a rural inn painted a golden hue that called out for further inspection. The owner had also once walked the camino, *and he took compassion on me. He just happened to have an extra room that he made available, and he kindly offered to drive me back to a restaurant I had already passed but which was the only place serving meals in the later afternoon. I took him up on his offer. Once again, my lodging issue was resolved and I was able to rest and eat well. I wondered, why do I waste time in worry?*

To advance innovation among faith-based nonprofits, we keep looking for unique opportunities. For several years, we hosted an annual awards ceremony to honor the year's freshest plans for outreach. The R. L. Petersen Awards for Non-Profit Innovation financially rewarded charities that took risks to extend themselves in creative ways. However, our initiative did more than that. We discovered that the sector also needed an excuse to gather and celebrate these risks, and our annual event became a means to do so. Publicly honoring these innovative organizations was an important way to reinforce our own philanthropic priorities, but we also believe it served the sector by keeping the need for innovation continually before organizational leaders.

Over the years, several nominees were recognized for their innovation, including:

- The Wellspring Foundation for Education's *Rwanda Teacher Training Project*, an initiative that leveraged the expertise of a high-quality private school in Kigali by sharing its best practices with government-funded teachers in twenty-two other schools throughout the country of Rwanda through weekend seminars and training. Not only did this project generously share its institutional learning but it also spread good will to public schools and educators who severely lacked professional development opportunities in an impoverished system. As a result, the nation's Ministry of Education designated Wellspring as a key partner in capacity building for the Rwandan educational system. To us, that was exceptional leverage.

- A Rocha Canada's *Environmental Education for Youth Project* partnered with four camps across Canada, impacting more than 12,000 children and teens with guided learning in environmental studies and the sharing of a love for nature. This new initiative helped spread the expertise of a small, new organization to camp staff and campers from three provinces, thus disseminating more broadly the organization's knowledge. We loved seeing small organizations grow their awareness and stretch their impact across the country to new constituencies.

- International Justice Mission Canada's *Justice for Bolivia Project* was launched by the Canadian organization as a way of developing its own programming arm, independent of its US parent, and established an operational field presence in the capital of La Paz. This start-up office provided effective legal investigation, intervention, and counseling services to street children and women and child victims of physical assaults, harassment, extortion, and illegal detention. The development of these program competencies was an important milestone in the maturation of the Canadian entity.

- Media Voice Generation's *Airtime Purchase Project* acquired national, Sunday morning airtime on Global TV to increase the exposure of a faith-based current affairs program to an audience ten times greater than the exposure of its previous time slot. This increased national profile led to host Lorna Dueck being approached by Toronto's *The Globe and Mail* to author a regular column on faith matters, and to frequently moderate heated online forums on spirituality on the Canadian Broadcasting Corporation's website.

- International China Concern's *Community Outreach Project* created new programming to provide caregiver support and training to families with severely disabled children in the regional capital of Changsha, China. Programming would better equip families to nurture their children within their own home contexts in contrast to prevailing cultural practices which frequently led parents to abandon severely disabled children at the hospital's doors to become wards of state-run institutions. Finding ways to move beyond traditional operating environments to creative new outreach formats was always appealing.

Each of these innovative organizations has something in common—a commitment to organizational growth and creative expansion, and the development of new programming to achieve their missions better.

The theory behind funding these sorts of projects is to empower an organization to stay on the leading edge of change and innovation, and more relevantly achieve the organization's mission. By partnering on these projects, we've been able to lead change, stir enthusiasm for the organization's work, and frequently witness these initiatives forming the foundation of new fundraising initiatives that are sustained on an ongoing basis by the organization's core donors. What starts on the unconventional edges of the organization's programming ends up moving to the center of their organizational focus.

Organizations that rely on donation revenue are typically constrained when it comes to funding unique, experimental initiatives outside their core program focus. Yet these experiments are the very types of projects that give the organization a hopeful future as it continues to expand services outward to meet its mission. Innovative projects are often ways toward organizational renewal, as older, stagnant program offerings are folded and new ones are launched. Funding innovation is usually directed toward growing organizations, ones that can handle the growth and expanded presence that the risk of these changes requires.

Funding innovation is also appropriate for major donors for several reasons. First, larger donors are able, in one act of generosity, to fund the launch of a new initiative that would take significant time and skill to communicate to an organization's smaller donors. In doing so, the organization risks diluting their effectiveness and focus by diverting core donors to new initiatives—the risk is great that core programming would be cannibalized by these new projects. There is considerably less risk in allowing an entrepreneurially minded major donor the opportunity to partner with the charity in this way.

Second, isolating new projects and allowing their sponsorship by one or a few major donors allows for a hothouse environment where the pilot project can be nurtured and refined before more general release to core donors after a period of time. Getting behind innovation is something that comes naturally to first-generation major donors who have often made their wealth through taking the risks inherent in innovation. These projects feel more natural to this constituency as they are an extension of their own personal ethos of "no risk, no reward."

While innovative projects can be birthed on the fringe of an organization's mission, they must be intentionally moved to the programming center in order for the new expansion or project to be sustainable through donation revenue. Often challenge or matching conditional grants are used by large donors to attract other donations. This is a method successfully used by many major donors to stimulate giving by the general public towards a charity's new programming. In doing so, they build up a cohort of donors who are captivated by the new initiative, and own its future success.

Conversations for your pilgrimage

1. If you were able to balance out your giving portfolio to include both blue chip and an array of riskier donations, what percentage would you assign to the riskier ones?

2. How appropriate is funding innovation for your philanthropy?

20

Beginning in isolation

Colunga (Day 19)

I launched out on my own again this morning without breakfast—Spaniards consider waking and eating prior to eight o'clock to be unheard of. My albergue offered a hot, served breakfast, but I decided not to wait for them to open. No worries, I told the owner, I would find a coffee place in Ribadesella. After an hour's walk, it would be open.

With great expectations (and growing hunger), I found an open café that had an espresso machine turned on. I was the sole customer, and after serving me, the male owner sat with two female employees and engaged in an animated discussion. After a few minutes I couldn't help but tune in, and then later tune out—he was rudely yelling at them, berating them for poor performance and a multitude of other ills. To my surprise, they were giving it back to him (I'm sure they were related), but it was a shameful performance that continued in an excruciating fashion for the full fifteen minutes it took me to drink my coffee. I could barely imagine an equivalent situation in Canada, and I was embarrassed to have to witness it.

Shaking off that negative experience, the coastal way opened up and I was treated to fantastic views for the rest of the day's walk. It was a Sunday in July, and Spaniards had flocked to the beach, creating an impossible traffic jam as too many cars tried to find parking. Most people, it seemed, were making a day of it—on the grassy side to the left of my path I saw picnics: improvised tables made with coolers, folding fabric chairs, and tarps strung overhead for shade, and on the sandy side to the right were the swimmers:

towels, surfboards, sunscreen, and, usually, bathing suits. I was surrounded by swarms of people, but walked a lonely path between the groups.

The last hour of the day, I turned inland, grateful to finally leave the circus of holidaymakers by the sea. Today was my last day for the ocean. For nineteen days I had hugged the coastline; now I began moving in a southwesterly direction away from the sea, through the mountains, to Santiago.

BAR - RESTAURANTE
Hostal - EL MESON -
Plaza Santa Ana - Teléf. 585 63 35
COLUNGA - ASTURIAS

As strange as it may sound, one of the common realities experienced by philanthropists is an unsettling isolation and the reality of being alone. In society's top 1 percent and buffered by wealth, it seems we don't need anyone. Family dynamics, always complicated, become more so when large amounts of money are thrown into the mix. For wealthy people of faith who belong to local churches, the place that is typically their cherished community can also become a challenging environment if they are its largest, not-so-anonymous donor. Despite this loneliness, we insulate our isolation further with lifestyle choices unavailable to most of our potential community.

Another cause of isolation is due to the philanthropist's generosity itself. Because of her giving, a philanthropist becomes sought after to host events, attend fundraisers, or go for lunches, coffees, and dinners. Fundraisers seek to cultivate relationship in order to acquire more funds for their charity, which can lead to an inauthenticity around interactions. The philanthropist finds himself questioning people's motives, being uncertain about the nature of their friendships, and being cautious about inviting new people into their lives. Who, truly, is my friend?

As the 2008–2009 recession decimated portfolios and began to impact charitable giving, I joined a conference call with a cross-section of executives affiliated with the private foundation peer group, Philanthropic Foundations Canada. What drew us to the call was the topic: "Managing your foundation in turbulent times."

Our board had gone through our own brutal reality check in early 2009, and these were indeed turbulent times. It arrived at some sobering conclusions regarding our philanthropic giving for the year. The board announced that all giving—both new grants and pledged amounts—were suspended for the remainder of the year, with pledged grants being postponed to the next year. They believed this hiatus would allow sufficient time for our portfolio to recover. Fortunately, the history of our giving ensured that we had accumulated a significant over-subscription towards our disbursement quota as required by the Canada Revenue Agency, so this overage could be applied toward what we were required to disburse in our fallow year.

With my colleagues on the line, I shared my perspective: when your grantmaking is reduced, it forces you to reevaluate your activity and reassess the value of what you do. A foundation may find their financial resources depleted, but it still has many other "assets" it can offer its charity partners. These include: advice, skills, companionship, networks, and faith.

In that fallow year when we took a pause from granting and suspended regular activity, we indeed discovered that the qualities that have shaped our grantmaking are what remains to be shared with our partners. Being generous is a state of mind, not an amount of money. We don't stop being generous because we lack resources; in their place, other gifts can be given. There was much to be found during this period of retrenchment, and it led us towards a model where we would no longer give alone, but learn to give as a community.

From this period of isolation, we ended up developing a process that would bring us together and bridge us with others. This was the beginning of what we would call Stronger Together.

Conversations for your pilgrimage

1. Have you felt isolated in your grantmaking?

2. How could you counter this dilemma?

21

Becoming stronger together

Valdedios (Day 20)

Today's lonely walk was a long twenty-eight kilometers but, oddly, it seemed short. I felt like I was flying, this even despite getting lost and adding an extra unnecessary loop of two kilometers. My route today took me off the Camino del Norte, and onto a connecting path to Oviedo that would eventually link me to the beginning of the Camino Primitivo, the original and oldest of all the caminos in Spain.

It was unusual that I had energy today, because, once again, I missed any sort of breakfast. Leaving at seven o'clock, I walked for an hour before I stopped for water and dried biscuits I had purchased the evening before. I had no coffee until midday when I arrived in the town of Villaviciosa. By then all I wanted was caffeine and a small bocadillo de tortilla. *Soon after, I came to the fork in the road where one yellow arrow painted in the pavement pointed me toward Oviedo and the start of the Camino Primitivo while another one indicated the continuation of the Camino del Norte along the sea. Both options led to Santiago, but it was a question of if you wanted mountains or coast. I chose mountains. The two paths diverged, and the coast slowly disappeared behind me.*

I arrived at Valdedios by mid-afternoon, not really knowing what to expect. In the middle of nowhere lay a remote Cistercian monastery built around a small rural church constructed in 899 AD. The adjacent monastery had been constructed in the thirteenth century. These fragments of belief and faithfulness had preserved Christian witness in the Iberian Peninsula for over eight centuries of Moorish occupation.

When I arrived, the whole monastery was shut down, save for the front gate, which was open. There were no monks in sight. I walked into the court-yard, but the various doors to the extensive buildings were all locked, with a sign saying to wait until four o'clock for someone to open the albergue. I was exhausted so I lay down outside the church using my backpack for a pillow. My cellphone had limited reception for Facebook but I was able to connect with Karen who was in the middle of a training session with a group of female NGO leaders in Phnom Penh. Could the juxtaposition of our lives be any stranger?

A commotion at the door of the albergue suddenly revealed I was not alone. A solitary Slovenian pilgrim had preceded me, and had already been admitted. It turned out we would be the only two to arrive at the monastery for the night. Katjuša let me in, and I was grateful to be able to find a bed and get cleaned up.

After a nap, I emerged outside and found her sitting on a low wall, writing in her journal. We began chatting, and within minutes found our-selves sharing deeply. The camino seemed to do that. Pilgrims were thrust together on a common journey, defenses were down, and we were hungry for community. Where else in life can you find yourself flung together with someone of such a different cultural background and life stage? The identi-ties we carefully manufacture back home were irrelevant; we were two hu-man beings pausing on a journey and stranded for the evening at this quiet monastery. For the next three hours, with no pressures to go anywhere or be anything, Katjuša and I traded stories, opinions, dreams, and longings. She was a young Italian-as-a-Second-Language teacher struggling to make ends meet. I was a philanthropist with resources. But we connected because we shared the same path; we were both pilgrims headed to a shared destination. Formerly alone along the Way, we now linked up as friends.

Growing hungry, our only source of food was across the road. We found the café owner boosting his dead car battery and discovered he did double duty as the caretaker for the monastery. Over dinner he enthusiastically showed us a binder full of historical documents tracing the history of this place. While we ate, a stray cat pressed up against my legs under the table, begging for pieces of shrimp from my paella with plaintive cries. Strangely, in all that time, we never saw any monks.

With an abundance of time suddenly on our hands created by the economic downturn, we thrust ourselves into a review of activities and an evaluation of our work. A surprising awareness dawned on our team: we were replete with assets beyond the financial. We were endowed with an astonishing array of networks, relationships, and experience. These too could be intentionally leveraged to help us achieve our goal of serving charities. By mid-2009, some exciting and unconventional opportunities began to formulate.

Our path forward would include other grantmakers. We developed a goal to more than triple our impact and allow for a similar level of granting towards capacity building projects as we had previously had in years when we were flush with cash. Not only that, but we quickly saw how coming together with others of like mind would benefit all of us with shared information, tools, processes, personnel, as well as the intangible sense of community that could emerge through intentionally working together on a project.

Initial conversations with fifteen colleagues led to mutual commitment by eight of us to form what we would eventually call Stronger Together 2010. As a group, we would offer $1 million in grants toward projects that would strengthen the ability of charities to weather tough economic times through funding core projects designed to reinforce and improve charity operations.

In the late fall, we began marketing Stronger Together 2010, seeking applications from eligible charities. By January, applications started to trickle in . . . but slowly. Had we made a colossal mistake? It was only at the deadline at the end of February that the applications rushed in. Comically (to us) our deadline just happened to occur the evening of the final, glorious USA-Canada men's gold medal hockey game of the Vancouver Olympics. Even during the game, applications kept arriving. By the time

Sidney Crosby had scored the winning overtime goal, the applications tallied 131—many more than I had wagered in our office pool.

My colleagues, Brent Fearon and Linda Dzelme, and I then began the colossal process of organizing these materials and presenting them to the granting partners for consideration. While this volume was daunting, we had the tools and processes in place to facilitate the task and we were eager to work hard. Applications were uploaded to a shared private website for viewing by all. Using a ranked scoring system based on our priorities, we were able to reduce the number of applications that would be considered in depth to a more manageable forty-nine.

Over the ensuing weeks, Brent and I divided responsibilities, and personally visited each of these short-listed applicants, of which a healthy percentage were new to us. Our dashboard and narrative evaluation for each organization's strengths and challenges was attached to the application, and allowed the granting partners to consider in detail the benefits of collaborating on these projects. We held our collective breath. This was a new and experimental process as collaboration by grantmakers was a novel and untested process. Though we were joined by a common faith, each one had distinct priorities and definite points of view. Would our system work? Would conflict erupt? Would our hard work bear fruit?

The moment of truth arrived. We gathered together with anticipation for a retreat in late spring at a hotel in Banff National Park, our discussions graced by an unbelievably majestic view of Lake Louise and the Rockies just outside our window. Over two days we discussed the merits and pitfalls of each application, and in the end chose to financially partner with forty-three organizations.

The decision-making process during the retreat was remarkable. The relaxed, two-day process encouraged partnerships and communication among us. Each donor had pledged a different amount. Committed funds from the eight donors were not pooled, so that each one retained control of their funding and made their own decisions according to their own priorities. This was one of the keys to our success. Philanthropy is an intensely personal expression of values and interests, and to pool funds of major donors would detract from the individual buy-in and commitment each grantmaker could make to a charity.

During this process, grantmakers considered each application and then indicated their interest in participating in the grant. Brent had created an Excel-based spreadsheet tool that we projected overhead to divide the total grant request by the pro-rated amounts remaining for each do-nor. Each one could view in real time their potential contribution and the amounts each one had remaining in their total pledge. Partners opted in or out on each grant according to their interest or ability.

A few weeks later, grants were announced. The Stronger Together 2010 partnership focused on capacity building funding, and grants awarded were destined for specific initiatives designed by the charity and corresponding to each one's unique needs. A wide variety of grants were awarded totaling $1,034,800, with the forty-three winning projects focused on marketing, fundraising, IT, digital media, administrative staffing, physical infrastruc-ture, strategic planning, or organizational realignment. Each organization pledged to report back to the group twice during the twelve-month term.

This collaborative venture offered several compelling benefits to par-ticipating grantmakers, including:

- Most of the grantmakers did not have staff, and were grateful for the philanthropic services we were able to offer. Our ability to conduct due diligence for each application with face-to-face interviews, along with our experience in assessment meant they could be more confi-dent of positive outcomes.

- Each grantmaker was exposed to charities that were new to them, al-lowing an easy entry point to gauge deeper involvement later.

- As we shared the burden of large grants, our individual contributions were small but multiplied many times by the participation of others in the grant. We shared the risk, and greatly leveraged the power of our own contributions.

- The isolation many major donors feel was offset as a community of grantmakers was established, trust was built, and communication was shared.

- Some donors deeply yearn for anonymity, or at minimum are pleased to have a third party to handle communications between themselves and potential charities. This protection was offered as a feature of our program, and some of our grantmakers appreciated the ability to stay off the radar.

As we circled around the table during the last day of the grant-ing retreat, each participant was asked for impressions and feedback.

Overwhelmingly, each person agreed that it was a worthwhile process, and each one indicated an interest in repeating the process in the future.

Our Stronger Together grants process has continued in every year since 2010. Each year the size of available grants and the number of grantmakers varies. But over the subsequent six years we collectively were able to grant over $5.2 million to 118 faith-based charities. Another million is being made available this year as I write.

Over the course of Stronger Together grants, we refined aspects of the program, and have learned much. In particular, we have streamlined the original process, so that grantmakers are not overwhelmed by large numbers of applications to consider. Instead they rely on our expertise to create a shortlist of high impact, innovative projects. They still have the final say, but we are able to cull the pool so that they only need to consider the best options for their philanthropy.

Another modification has been to increase the size of the grants. We find we tend to conduct the same level of due diligence whether a grant is $10,000 or $100,000. Zeroing in on larger healthy organizations that are seeking larger grants ensures that Stronger Together grants typically reach their targets and fulfill the aspirations of the grantmakers for high-impact funding. With our intensive level of due diligence, it was not cost effective to spend time analyzing the viability of smaller requests.

Finally, the emphasis of Stronger Together grants has shifted over time. Initially we experimented with different granting focuses—from capacity building to partnerships between charities—but we eventually landed on innovation as being the key theme of these grants. As mentioned previously in the chapter on innovation, we believe such grants are especially positioned to jump-start creative outreach by charities. An investment into innovation will continue to be a hallmark of Stronger Together grants moving forward.

Conversations for your pilgrimage

1. How can your philanthropy be maximized by working with others?

2. Would you consider joining with others in a collaborative grants process?

22

Creative collaboration

Pola de Siero (Day 21)

Staying at a monastery in an isolated valley was not the idyllic spiritual experience I had imagined. I slept poorly and dreamed vividly. The hungry cat from our evening meal across the road had followed us back, but we had locked her out. She meowed through the night at the door, her desperately annoying cries echoing through the wide, cold, stone hallways. In the fogginess of sleep, I was aware of the meows growing louder; she must have found a way in. Then, with an unexpected pounce, the cat landed on me as I slept. Startled, I swatted it away; she retreated to the kitchen where she scattered dry pasta all over the floor.

When morning dawned, a steep thirty-minute grind up out of the valley greeted me, but once I ascended, the views from the top of the ridge were incredible. The monastery lay nestled in a crevasse, and the early yellow sun gave the view a spectacular, golden haze.

Today's solo walk would be a shorter eighteen kilometers to the city of Pola de Siero. After the initial climb, the remaining walk led me through villages and rolling landscape until I reached the city. It was a much larger urban center than I had expected, and upon entering I soon lost sight of arrows that guided me to the church and albergue. I found myself in the city market, and pulled out my guidebook. The closest lodging was a small hotel. Rather than spend more time searching for the albergue, I checked in. Feeling the need to be a little bit civilized, I found my way to a laundromat and a barber, resulting in clean clothes and a haircut.

Strategy

The next day I would end this transitional path, and arrive in Oviedo where the Camino Primitivo began. I didn't realize it, but my camino was about to shift from coastal mountains and solitary walking, to higher mountains and the beginning of a camino family.

Collaborative efforts by grantmakers can also be undertaken with charities. One such project was what we called the 35<35 Project. Inspired by other initiatives that identified younger leaders in order to honor their creativity and drive, a group of organizations felt it worthwhile to do the same for faith-based younger leaders in the nonprofit sector. Again, this initiative was birthed through existing relationships where confidence in one another was already present. Carson Pue from Arrow Leadership, John Pellowe from the Canadian Council of Christian Charities, Doug Koop from *Christian Week*, and I gathered to consider this initiative.

Each partner offered strengths the others lacked: Arrow Leadership brought its extensive experience in identifying leaders and offering leadership development opportunities, the CCCC offered broad awareness of the faith-based charitable sector in Canada along with a well-attended annual conference where the younger leaders could be identified, *Christian Week* supplied the mechanism by which the leaders were to be profiled through a color insert in its biweekly newspaper as well as the ability to write the content, and our foundation offered its funding capability.

Through a lengthy application process, the project identified thirty-five remarkable emerging leaders between eighteen and thirty-five who were impacting their communities with excellence. It has been fascinating to follow these leaders as time as progressed. They included such people as Kirk Giles of Burlington, Ontario, who now leads Promise Keepers with outreach to men, Jenna Smith, a community leader at Christian Direction in Montreal, and Karla Adolphe, a brilliant and passionate folk musician and songwriter from High River, Alberta.

In another example, in 2015 we tried a new type of collaborative effort, one that resulted in some significant outcomes for charitable work in Canada. I was approached by Frontier Marketing Company, a small firm based in Victoria, British Columbia, led by Ben Johnson, to consider working with them and with the Seacrest Foundation from Vancouver. It would be the first time we would try a unique partnership with a business.

The purpose of this initiative was to highlight the lack of attention many charities place on online fundraising, and to demonstrate that concerted effort using expert consultants could reap substantial dividends for these charities. The three partners coordinated funding and resources to develop a study of online giving among Canadian Christian charities, and a subsequent matching campaign done with the assistance of Frontier.

The research is available online and was published as *A Transformation in Online Giving.*[1] It analyzed publicly available website, social media, and CRA data from over fifty Canadian Christian charities, and interpreted a user's experience (how easy to donate, how many clicks to donate, how soon until acknowledgement/receipt, etc.), how many and which charities use what tools or third-party programs, social media presence and usage, and more.

Digital matching campaigns were developed for six inner city missions by Frontier Marketing Company, and we offered $10,000 in matching funds to each organization to attract their donors to giving. We counter-intuitively conducted the match during the sleepy summer months when most donors are on holiday, in order to demonstrate that the Frontier campaign could capture the imaginations of each charity's donors. What transpired surprised us all: in a two-week period of using Frontier's expertise, our $60,000 was multiplied four more times by the six selected charities' donors.

We were learning that doing philanthropy in isolation was like addition, but collaborating with others, even with partners unlike ourselves, was like multiplication. Greater leverage and impact occurs through these sorts of creative partnerships. Once again we proved that together we are stronger.

---

1. You can download this report at http://www.digitalcharity.ca.

Strategy

Conversations for your pilgrimage

1. Who are possible partners for you in creative collaboration?
2. How can your giving move from addition to multiplication?

23

Journeying with beneficiaries

Oviedo (Day 22)

The camino is a psychological journey as much as a physical one. Last evening alone in the city, I realized how much I was craving people as the demands of this walk begin to wear on me. Katjuša, the Slovenian at the monastery, was the only pilgrim I had seen or talked to in several days but even she had now disappeared.

This morning started out wet, and didn't improve throughout the day. My poncho flapped in the wind, moist plastic adhering to my legs as I walked. As I was still transiting between the Norte and Primitivo stages, I didn't have accurate maps showing the camino; to compensate, I decided to walk along the highway toward Oviedo. I guessed that at the next town, the roundabout would reconnect me to the path again.

As I approached the junction, an unusual pilgrim emerged in the mist, clad in jeans and a damp, black hoodie, lugging an enormous backpack, and bearing two large wooden staffs with curious markings, carvings, and ribbons festooning them. He was clearly not the typical hiker equipped with the latest gear. I greeted him, and we began chatting as we walked. Léo was a twenty-four-year-old French pilgrim from Paris who had walked all the way from Mont-St-Michel on the Breton coast. He had been walking for two months, most of it in solitude; he reminded me of my son, Nate, in that he was clearly listening to the beat of a different drummer.

As we walked and talked—for Léo was as desperate as I was for company—we began to overtake another pilgrim in a voluminous red poncho. Léo remarked that it was a Slovenian woman he had just met. I realized it was Katjuša, whom I had befriended two nights earlier. We reconnected warmly and walked for a bit together, but soon she begged us to move on ahead as she was walking slowly, favoring a sore ankle.

Still in the countryside, Léo noticed an open church, so we popped in for a look and a chance to dry off. The church was one of those twelfth-century beauties that was loaded with character and could tell so many stories. We climbed the tower, squeezing single file up the passage just wide enough for my shoulders. As we descended, Katjuša appeared at the doorway for her own look, but we moved on ahead.

We advanced, approaching the urban fringe of Oviedo. The more we walked, the more Léo talked in his dramatic French-accented English. By now the rain had started coming down in earnest. Popping into a bar, we ordered coffees, and as we finished, who should appear across the street adjusting her poncho but Katjuša. I called her in and we drank a second round of coffees together and planned for the evening. The camino was odd like that—we felt like we were being pulled together, as if the camino itself had a personality, and was actively adjusting our lives to enable relationships.

Léo and I decided to walk on ahead, pledging to meet Katjuša at the albergue, not realizing at the time that the two listed in our guidebooks were now closed, and another one not listed had recently opened. This led to some redundant walking in circles and inquiring of passersby the way to the new albergue. The center of Oviedo was beautiful—an old Spanish city, laden with history as the capital of Asturias, Oviedo is the seat of the principality whose prince is heir to the throne of Spain. The downtown cathedral was the original starting point for the Camino Primitivo, the first of all the caminos that are woven through Spain. Outside the church was a plaque embedded in the pavement stating that King Alfonso II began the tradition in the ninth century when he chose to walk to Santiago to pray.

We found Katjuša in the new albergue—a seminary—and she invited Léo and me to join her for dinner along with two others she had met: a Greek woman, Kiriaki, and Jacques from Montpellier. It was a beautiful dinner, full of laughter, relaxed fun, and zany conversation. After dinner we returned to the albergue where people began settling in for the night. Léo and I found a patch on the ground outside the albergue and swapped stories while others slept. He was a fascinating nomad, a young man on a pilgrimage that would take him to Santiago and beyond. He was very intelligent, but disdainful of formal education. He planned to walk beyond Santiago to Finisterre—the "end of the world" located ninety kilometers beyond Santiago at the Atlantic Ocean, where Europe ran out and the Americas were the next landmass. From Finisterre he intended to hitchhike to Andalucía, and find a cargo ship to carry him to South America.

The benefits of collaboration are also evident when we walk together with beneficiaries of our philanthropy. It is surprising and humbling to take this leap when we realize that our money does not have the final word. Indeed, there is so much that we can gain from entering into relationship with those unlike ourselves. Journeying together comes when we can surrender our sole identity as "givers" and learn to also become "receivers," acknowledging a mutuality of relationship.

We found an excellent charity partner when we discovered Opportunity International as it launched in Canada at the turn of the century. Opportunity offers microfinance loans, insurance, and training to the entrepreneurial poor, and it is built upon a model which encourages mutual learning between donors and recipients. As a volunteer board member for eight years, I had the privilege of drilling deep into its model and seeing firsthand their stellar work in countries throughout Latin America, Asia, and Africa.

Due to our background as missionaries in the beautifully complicated country of Colombia, we have a special affinity for that nation and its resilient, generous people. However, Opportunity's work in Colombia by Canadians was nonexistent until we spearheaded expansion there in collaboration with Bogotá-based Jim Frantz, Canadian vice president Doris Olafsen, and program director Martha Arias.

Opportunity became the pathway for us to directly connect with the poor in barrios around Colombia's major cities such as the port of Cartagena. Cartagena de Indias was known as *La Heróica* (The Heroic One) because for 500 years the city withstood attacks from ruthless pirates of the Caribbean, blockades by the imperial British navy, and the tragedies of over fifty years of civil war fought by leftist guerrillas, right-wing paramilitaries, government forces, and narcotraffickers. Cartagena's fortifications and immense walls have stood the test of time, and weatherworn cannons still point outward to the harbor.

But a greater battle outside the tourist zone was being fought against the grinding poverty that grips the majority of the city's million-plus inhabitants. One day I walked through Olaya barrio, accompanied by Opportunity's Colombian staff. The heavy humidity and heat of the tropics birthed a line of sweat on my upper lip. A fat sow wallowed in the black, stagnant, disease-filled waters that flow outside homes down the unpaved street. Toddlers, barefoot and clad only in soiled underpants, stood staring blankly in the doorways of the homes.

We paused at one humble doorway, and I steeled myself before crossing the threshold. But inside, remarkably, I discovered my first Cartagena hero. Graciela sat with an open, worn Bible on her lap, thick reading glasses resting in the fold, lines from the Psalms underlined in blue ink. When I asked what she had been reading, she spoke with confidence and conviction, and her face glowed. Only God could help her live day by day; he gave her hope despite the misery of her surroundings. Graciela told me about her small convenience store that sold goods to the community; she was on her fifth Opportunity loan cycle. Her first loan was $200; she now had a $500 loan she would pay off faithfully over the next sixteen weeks. And she was a saver, able with her growing business to regularly put small amounts away for the rainy day, which in this barrio would be inevitable.

Graciela got up, securing her wooden door with a padlock and chain, and accompanied us to Manuel's home next door. In that instant, I met my second hero. We stood together in his dirt-floor home while he stirred a huge vat of caramelizing milk, which, when reduced, becomes *arequipe*, a sticky-sweet caramel spread. He would fill small disposable containers and sell them for a dollar apiece, peddling them door to door. With the Opportunity loan that helped him establish this microbusiness, he was able to make ends meet for his family.

I couldn't resist, as the smell of burnt caramel in *arequipe* brought back a flood of memories. So I told Manuel my story. When our son was one and a half, we found him laughing hysterically in our Bogotá kitchen, painting our dog with a large spoon of this caramel spread. Our miniature pinscher was frantically racing in circles, his tongue hanging out, not quite reaching the sweetness, and attempting unsuccessfully to lick his back quarters clean. At the climax of my story, Manuel joined in laughing uproariously, his toothless grin full of life.

Our group increased as we walked down the street. Graciela and Manuel stuck to us just like that *arequipe*—it's not every day that your banker pays house calls. We appeared at the door of my third hero of the day.

Carmina was into everything. A riot of candy is what first beckoned my attention, but as our eyes focused on her store, we also saw school supplies arrayed behind a glass counter, three very used-looking computers (she charged kids to play games), a sign announcing cell phone rental for local calls at 200 pesos a minute, and a mail order catalogue business where she received a commission for household items purchased by the community. Her eleven-year-old daughter sat judiciously at the counter with a lined notebook, recording the time, date, length of call, and amount charged for the cell phone usage. Carmina's entrepreneurial spirit had propelled her into the presidency of her local Opportunity trust bank.

On that day I met three Cartagena heroes, three individuals who gave me a great gift. Meeting valiant and dignified people who resisted poverty through faith and through the simple hand up of a microloan filled me with hope in human resilience, the gift of being made in the image of God. It put my own life into proper perspective. Their gratitude humbled me. Their tenaciousness inspired me. The juxtaposition of a wealthy donor from a rich country plunked down into the world's worst misery is often emotionally devastating. But in doing so, I was taught a wonderful lesson: some of the most generous, wealthiest people I have ever met have been financially poor.

Returning from site visits where our comfortable world collides with the immense challenges of those who live on less than two dollars a day is not only humbling; it is a gift. We receive the experience and need to reflect deeply on the encounters, letting it impact our lives with prophetic truth. This leads us to simplify, advocate, and cultivate generosity with our own families and communities at home and beyond.

This insightful trip with Opportunity consolidated a significant grant we made to the efforts there: a million-dollar expansion for the work of launching the development of a formal financial institution created to serve the needs of the poor, and to jump-start Canadian donations to that country. By 2015 our original investment had been multiplied sixfold by others into realigning an economy at the grassroots. The new institution struggled through years of start-up woes during which we walked alongside. This required patience, forgiveness, sensitivity, and determination, but all along our investment was bolstered by confidence in the passion and ability of Opportunity's staff. Through frequent visits and close contact on the ground, we were able to partner with the financially poor, relationally wealthy heroes of Cartagena.

Conversations for your pilgrimage

1. Do you ever have the opportunity to engage with the grassroots beneficiaries of your philanthropy?

2. How have you been impacted by these encounters?

24

Learning in community

Grado (Day 23)

Another wet day dawned, and with twenty people crammed into ten bunk beds in a small room, staying quiet was nearly impossible in the lightening darkness. There was no ladder to the floor, so I cautiously stepped on the frame of the bed below, hoping not to jostle Katjuša. I heaved my backpack over my shoulder, lugging it into the hallway to sort its contents in the light before heading out.

I walked alone through the glistening streets of Oviedo as the city awoke. The misty rain soon soaked my face, but it made for cooler temperatures and it was a pleasure to walk, guided by brass scallop shells located in the sidewalks at every intersection. To my left, I saw the door of a small church surreptitiously open and close. Upon further inspection, I realized that an early morning mass was being held, so I entered. The church was packed with people beginning their work day, and I stood in the back with others who had arrived late.

Conventional wisdom states that religious faith in Europe is dead. But this regular workday morning, like many other times on my two caminos, convinced me otherwise. There will always be a remnant, a faithful fragment, who buck the trends of secularity, and continue to believe. I also perceived from my conversations with Léo and Katjuša that, though it is markedly different than past generations, a humble spirituality continues to be nurtured and thrives in the next generations.

Strategy

I exited Oviedo and began climbing, passing through small villages. At one stop, two young, enthusiastic Hungarian men stood outside a shrine with a cardboard placard listing the ingredients of homemade vegan energy bars they had made for pilgrims. For any donation, you could have one. I threw a euro in their hat and stuck one of the bars in my bag for when I needed that extra boost.

These Hungarians were just two of many new fresh-faced pilgrims I began to see on the path today. Oviedo is the official start of the Primitivo pilgrimage to Santiago, and, due to its length (twelve stages), fits better into the vacation schedules of most people. So in due course today, I walked alongside Lili, a Brazilian woman who had abandoned corporate life, Angel, a Madrileño who was still talking on his cell phone sorting out issues with his car's mechanic, and Pedro, an enthusiastically cheery physical education teacher from Andalucía who strode by everyone with his long legs and tireless energy.

I eventually stopped in the town of Grado and found a sweet, single room in a hostel that also offered pilgrims a set menu included in the price of lodging—a first course of fish soup, a second of chicken and fries, and an almond tart for dessert. Angel and Pedro were two of the familiar faces who showed up at dinner and shared the table.

Journeying together doesn't only mean developing a heart to listen and learn from the voices of those we help. For our philanthropy to become even stronger, we must learn to break down the walls that exist between ourselves as funders. Too often there is a sense of isolation that pervades the work of philanthropy. We know other major donors contribute to the same organizations, but we tend to rarely speak to one another or to have a full awareness of the extent of our colleagues' grantmaking. Fundraisers who work for the charities and have done their research will have far better a grasp on the scope and nature of a donor's interests than will many of their peers. But if donors are collaborating financially on the same project with the same organization, it makes sense for relationships to form and exchange of information to occur.

Collaboration between funders is about more than relationships. Clear communication and trust within the funding community allows for greater understanding and effectiveness in the partnership with a charity. As a result, one of the questions in our grant application probes who the other project funders are in an effort to allow for a community to form and to have a sense of the ownership of the project. It also prevents the temptation to double-dip—where charities obtain funding from donors for the same project.

In our earlier years, we were drawn to The Gathering, the annual conference of evangelical grantmakers in the US, who unite for a few days in September for a highly anticipated conference filled with seminars on developing a great grantmaking program, inspiring plenary sessions on faith and giving, and lots of down time to connect with each other informally.

My friend, Fred Smith, the president of The Gathering, believes the relationships that form through this venue have created the basis for stronger and more courageous family philanthropy. Having the insights of one's peers applied to one's giving decisions allows for giving with greater conviction and passion.

Fred was also instrumental in the creation of another group years ago. While The Gathering focused on empowering wealthy families in their giving decisions, several felt an informal association of professional grantmakers who shared evangelical convictions and who were employees of large foundations was required. For years this group of friends would informally meet with each other to share ideas on how to give well. After time, it was decided that they needed a name, so they began swapping stories of worst grantmaking experiences. Fred told of the huckster who phoned him from a payphone off a rural Texas interstate, telling an implausible story of a pet pig who was used in gospel presentations and explaining that he needed $5 million to continue these outreach opportunities. Unsurprisingly, the guy never made it to Fred's office. But it did provide twisted inspiration for the name of this motley crew. We called ourselves "Pigs," and have become a group of professionals dedicated to great grantmaking, in honor of the worst philanthropic request in our history. Years later, one of our principals tired of this demeaning name, and we tried to clean it up by anointing our group the "Professionals in Grantmaking Society"—but the PIGS moniker for better or worse stuck for many years. The acronym reminds us to be humble.

A natural outflow of this kind of peer interaction is the opportunity to collaborate with others on projects of mutual interest. Each partner brings their strengths, connections, and insights to the table, and all are able to accomplish more together.

In recent years, we have grown increasingly aware of the need for a Canadian community for faith-based grantmakers. Greg Pennoyer and I have journeyed many miles together over the years, and one of our frequent topics of conversation has been what it would look like in Canada as we perceived the need for a more authentic expression of philanthropy partnership for Canadian Christians. Both of us were limited by our other responsibilities, but in recent years he has had the ability to dedicate a part of his time towards the development of The Roundtable.

The Roundtable is a membership association of Canadian grantmakers which offers intimate gatherings with high caliber speakers on diverse topics such as family philanthropy from one generation to the next, the intersection of faith and film, granting for impact, investing in social enterprise, and creating space to hear each other's stories. While this group is still in its infancy, it is growing as word gets out and members affiliate. A space is being created to grow together as we advance on the philanthropic journey. A community of philanthropy is intentionally being birthed, which makes us all better.

Conversations for your pilgrimage

1. In your philanthropy, do you walk alone or with others? What does walking with others look like to you?

2. How can your philanthropy be strengthened by entering into a community of peers?

Attitudes

Let us sing now, not in order to enjoy a life of leisure,
but in order to lighten your labors.
You should sing as wayfarers do—
sing, but continue your journey.
Do not be lazy, but sing
to make your journey more enjoyable.
Sing, but keep going.

– St. Augustine[1]

1. Norris, *The Cloister Walk*, 167.

25

Becoming proactive

Bodenaya (Day 24)

The forecast called for this to be the last day of rain. What a relief! On went the poncho again, and I stepped out, once again beginning alone. The first four kilometers were a long, slow climb but the view was breathtaking, with clouds languishing between the mountains, strung out like pearls. On the way down the other side, I spotted a familiar red poncho ahead, and as I caught up I recognized Katjuša and Kiriaki walking together. We continued on together and after a couple of hours stopped where, just off the side of the path in the middle of nowhere, some enterprising Spaniard had placed a Coke machine and a bench. As we munched on apples and chocolate, suddenly Léo appeared from around the bend. Though travelling separately and not seeing each other yesterday, being on the same path ensured we would keep converging as companions.

The four of us walked along together but the women walked at a slower pace, so Léo and I eventually moved on ahead, enjoying our conversation. After several hours we stopped in Salas for a beer and a pintxo. Salas was my intended stopping place for the day, but Léo and the women convinced me to push on ahead another seven kilometers. I agreed, not realizing it was a steep uphill grind most of the way. Getting to Bodenaya at the top of the mountain would mean a record walk of thirty-five kilometers.

Walking with someone gave me energy, and it was Léo who did most of the talking. Today he offered vehement political opinions on the French loss of sovereignty to the EU and the USA in his comic, heavily accented English. I could only grunt and sweat, but his nonstop rant kept us moving.

We finally arrived at a small, private hostel run by David, a Spaniard who had bought the house in February with the vision of making it a true sanctuary for the traveler. I had no reservation, but he offered me a bunk. He warmly welcomed us in with hot coffees and a generous offer to wash our clothes.

Twenty-one pilgrims would find this albergue *their home for the evening. I sat on the retaining wall outside the entrance, inspired as each of them trickled in, completely spent from the climb and needing to rest, foul moods instantly softened by genuine, caring hospitality. We were drawn together around the table for a simple family meal of pasta and salad, then a great vegetarian soup prepared by David with produce from his garden. All over the albergue were flags, pins, mementos, and badges given as thank-you gifts for the welcome he offered. This* albergue *followed the spirit of the* camino *and didn't charge for lodging and meals; instead, pilgrims contributed what they could. I planned to give a generous contribution the next morning.*

Many generous people develop a reactive approach to their philanthropy—waiting for charities to approach them before they decide to participate. I don't blame anyone for this approach: it is, frankly, often overwhelming to be a public-facing major donor. Such a donor is exposed and the target of many persistent and worthwhile requests of time, attention, and money. It's tough work to narrow one's scope, and it's hard to say no.

As well, in family philanthropy there are often many competing interests within the family that vie for consideration. I believe being reactive stems from an inability within the family system to zero in on a proactive strategy with a defined and clear purpose. Many families lack the ability to speak frankly about their philanthropy together. Often, the second and third generations defer to the founders' vision, with their own perspectives given little consideration. If a founder wishes their foundation to continue in perpetuity, he or she must inclusively draw in and listen to the voices from next generations early on rather than trying to control the agenda from the grave.

Some families react by closing the doors on meeting with anyone, or by creating huge barriers that will dissuade all but the most ingenious development staff. It is a natural and common reaction if organizing philanthropy and creating a strategy going forward has not occurred.

The result of this reaction will be a scattered and haphazard approach to philanthropy based on whims of the moment, obligations at the end of the year, and the relational strengths of the fundraisers. For years we operated under the framework of sitting back and waiting for grantseekers to discover us, rather than determinedly moving ahead with a plan to seek out potential partners to help us fulfill our own grantmaking strategy. Unfortunately, this led to a series of unsatisfying and less effective grants as funding ended up going to the most persistent fundraisers, not the most creative opportunities.

An opposite approach is that of being proactive. My friend, Emily Neilsen Jones, in Boston, is an excellent example. Her foundation, the Imago Dei Fund, intentionally collaborates with faith-based charities that advance equality for women in leadership in the church and in society. She writes columns and passionate blog posts, she selects organizational partners that exemplify and advance the values she holds, she tirelessly pushes resistant Christian organizations to expand their concepts of equality, and exposes patriarchal perspectives in her interactions with charity leaders. Her foundation has become more than just a funding vehicle—she is an active agent for change.

Defined values, process, and strategy provide the necessary boundaries which allow a funder to pursue charitable partners without fearing being overwhelmed by the demands of approaches that have no resonance with their direction. The better articulated a strategy, the more proactive we can become in our grantmaking.

I became proactive rather than reactive when we zeroed in on our giving priorities for innovation and capacity building. One particular instance from 2006 comes to mind, one which resulted in significant impact in Afghanistan. I met with John Kelsall, then president of Montreal-based

Health Partners International Canada (HPIC), and his colleague, Christine Lancing, at a coffee shop near my home. We were ready to explore a new initiative together, having recently completed a successful grant in Cuba.

We began talking about the war in Afghanistan—our involvement as a nation had intensified with Canada committing significant troops in the toughest corner of the country, and news about Kandahar was in the papers daily. And yet, humanitarian aid was also required to demonstrate a commitment to ordinary people affected by this conflict. I asked how they were involved. Unfortunately, they told me that HPIC had no local partners who could assist in accomplishing its mission in that country.

Through my networks, I saw an opportunity. A friend, Craig Hammon, was executive vice president for CURE International, based in Pennsylvania. Craig had told me about the CURE International Hospital in Kabul, and had been encouraging me to accompany him to visit his work there. Until then I had turned him down. With no Canadian charitable partner, it hadn't previously been realistic for us to consider involvement. Now HPIC's involvement as a Canadian charity partner for CURE suddenly opened our options.

HPIC excels at sourcing donated pharmaceuticals from Canadian drug companies, and shipping them to places in need. For larger projects, they fill whole containers and deliver them to nations as required. One of their ongoing challenges, however, is assuring themselves that the donated drugs and supplies actually reach those they intend to assist. The prospect of having an on-the-ground partner like CURE as the public face of distribution for these resources, together with our financing of the project made for an excellent synergistic relationship. Within months the initiative took wing.

Over 113,000 Afghans would ultimately benefit from this two-year project. Being on the ground in Kabul with a trusted local partner also provided HPIC with needed credibility when the Canadian government sought NGO partners in the country to complement its military presence. As a result of HPIC's humanitarian intervention at the right place and time, they were successful in securing a $5 million contract with the Canadian International Development Agency (CIDA) to continue its work for several years beyond our grant. Many more hundreds of thousands of Afghans were assisted, and HPIC was called out in the House of Commons as an exemplary charitable partner for the Canadian government.

Our proactive approach at the right time was the key to allowing an organization to launch out with a new initiative that positioned it for significant growth and impact in future years. It allowed HPIC to be stretched to the margins of its capacity in offering health care for Afghans during a time of great need. Decisive action enabled our charitable investment to be leveraged many times over as it was multiplied by CIDA.

While we soon developed a strategy around our granting priorities focusing on the two streams of innovation and capacity building for Canadian Christian charities, I grew to realize that an even sharper focus was required for our grantmaking. We had a big heart for international giving by small and large charities doing grassroots work in demanding developing world contexts. Yet after a decade of these grants, I began analyzing our history and found that over that period we had given grants to projects in more than sixty different countries. For most of the larger grants, I personally visited sites and saw firsthand the results of our interventions. But it became physically impossible and a poor stewardship of funds to personally visit all of these far-flung sites.

An invitation from The Gathering was instrumental in helping us refine our focus. They had recently begun to offer insight trips so that major donors could be exposed to a particular issue to explore the possibility of leveraging wealth for greater impact. In 2010 they announced a trip to Cambodia, and Karen and I eagerly registered. Over a two-week period, fifteen of us met with dozens of national and international NGO leaders at work in Cambodia who were focused on the challenging issues around human trafficking.

One of our leaders during this exposure trip was Jeremy Floyd, a program officer for Equitas Group, a Knoxville-based foundation that had developed relationships and expertise in this area. Several of us on our insight trip began to acquire a vision for collaboration that was rooted in sincere friendship as fellow journeyers: Emily Neilsen Jones and Deb Veth from Imago Dei Fund, Aaron LeClaire from Cornerstone Trust, Jeremy, and me.

Since Jeremy's full-time focus was Cambodian NGOs, he quickly became a great resource for all of us. He knew all the local players, the intricate relationships between the charities, and the challenging issues around trafficking that well-intentioned grants could not easily resolve. There were dozens of big-hearted donors and humanitarian agencies at work in Cambodia, but we found that without coordination there was frequent overlap, and deeper, strategic issues were seldom addressed. Working together helped all of us give grants that became significant investments into moving a nation beyond easy aid.

One grant stands out. Together we collaborated to fund the creation of the Bachelor of Social Work degree program at the Royal University of Phnom Penh. This grant contravened our specific granting criteria on two counts: it was neither a Christian nor a Canadian charity. However, we reasoned that our proactive collaboration could fund a new generation of educated social workers, many of whom ended up working for Christian NGOs in Cambodia that were addressing the injustices of trafficking. I was convinced once I met with Dr. Tracy Harachi from the University of Washington in Seattle, who had pioneered this work with support from her institution. Under Jeremy's trusted guidance and ongoing hands-on involvement, we shared the risk with our foundation colleagues.

Despite being outside our normal framework, our proactivity was necessary, and the resulting outcomes were exceptional. In 2013, *The New York Times* profiled our initiative.[1] It was confirmation of the value of this endeavor when others saw and celebrated this new educational opportunity for rebuilding of social work in a country where any form of education had been decimated a generation previously.

This growing focus on Cambodia eventually led us to make many additional grants to charities at work in this country such as Ratanak International, Prison Fellowship, Asian Outreach, Chab Dai Coalition, FH Canada, World Relief Canada, and more. It also contributed to our own personal focus outside our own foundation work. Karen developed a specialized leadership development initiative for female Cambodian NGO leaders, resulting in specialized mentoring and capacity building for these gifted women for four sessions over two years. Her frequent trips to Cambodia from 2010 to the present is an intentional, longer-term investment into leadership upon which healthy social change is built. Our proactive focus on one particular area of emphasis permitted us greater satisfaction and understanding as to the long-term impact we could have as a foundation.

Conversations for your pilgrimage

1. Have you ever been proactive in granting? What have you learned in the process?

1. Gillet, "Cambodia," para. 5–7.

2. How would narrowing your focus make you a better grantmaker?

26

A call for greater openness

Campiello (Day 25)

The morning dawned as a German version of "Ave Maria" softly wafted through the albergue, stirring us from sleep. Then, as consciousness rose, we heard twelve-string Spanish guitars played with fantastic abandon from the Concierto de Aranjuez. The music transported me back twenty years to Colombia when I had purchased that same CD recording. (Back in those days, we had a limited CD collection of five recordings.) My stay in Bodenaya would stand out as the albergue most consistent with the spirit of the Way— generous community life outside the mainstream. It was inspiring and I was refreshed.

Léo and I walked together, and along the way were joined by Esben, a young Danish man who had also stayed at the Bodenaya albergue. Esben had a master's degree in philosophy and business administration, but was seeking a better way to live out his beliefs than within the restrictive framework of the corporation where he had worked.

The views were magnificent as we crested a forested ridge overlooking the valley below, though the rain of the past several days had wreaked havoc on the path. Mud and pools of water were everywhere. While the sun shone and began drying the goop, we focused on avoiding the largest sinkholes on the path.

We transited through the town of Tineo, then past a monastery, and stopped in the forest, sitting on the ground for a picnic lunch of chorizo, cheese, bread, and chocolate. Finally, by late afternoon we arrived in a village and I knew I had reached my limit today at twenty-six kilometers. Esben moved on ahead, but Léo stayed. He carried a tent, and planned to sleep in the open air. His limited budget prevented him from staying in the brand-new albergue that had just opened; at ten euros it seemed reasonable enough to me.

In a conversation with the owner and seeing a need, I offered to translate the detailed instructions for the albergue's new washer and dryer from Spanish to English, and Léo contributed a translation into French. With gratitude, our host unexpectedly offered us a free meal. The camino kept providing.

Foundations aren't known as the most transparent and accessible of organizations. There is something about the nature of giving—it is seen to be a private and personal decision—that somehow influences foundations in being opaque and want to fly under the radar. Individual giving to charity deserves to be treated as a confidential matter, but when a charity, church, foundation, corporation, or government gives to charitable causes, transparency should be the norm.

Why? Clarity and honesty in foundation-giving are important because of the amounts of funds that are being delivered. Unfortunately, money talks, and anonymous giving by large actors can obscure the rationale for decisions being made by a charity.

As well, foundations are a creation of public good will, and do not pay taxes on their income. The trade-off, therefore, is public accountability. Individuals who treat their private foundations as entities that do not need to be accountable to the public have not grasped the benefit that accrues to them by virtue of their tax-free status. Once the decision has been made to create a foundation, personal reluctance to divulge one's giving to charity needs to be abandoned. The left hand must know what the right hand is doing.

Technology is a great tool to encourage greater transparency. A public website, along with social media, including Facebook, Twitter, and

YouTube, as well as blogs and online forums, are an inescapable reality that bring to light what has previously been obscured. Engaging with these technologies will increasingly be demanded of foundations and other large formal givers.

Early in the maturing stage of Bridgeway's journey, we realized our need to open our doors and become visible. For a few years we had attempted, unsuccessfully, to keep our granting a secret and private affair. But understanding that our foundation's status was an expression of public trust led us to choose explicit accountability. Even the most resistant foundations must know that each of their grants is part of the public record and only a few clicks away on the CRA website.

Rather than try to hide our giving, we did what was counterintuitive, and brought our giving into the light. We preferred to define our foundation ourselves, rather than having it defined by others for us. We launched a website and became very open about our grantmaking process. Annual lists of our grants were posted and are available. We regularly featured a different partner charity each month on the website to highlight the best. We weren't trying to toot our own horn, but to be quietly transparent about what we were doing, and to serve charities by profiling their successes.

What this public openness did for us was surprising. As many other foundations have experienced, we used to receive piles of proposals, about one per day, some several inches thick complete with videos and DVDs, PowerPoint presentations, photos, handwritten letters, reference letters, and/or urgent pleas for help. It was beyond one person's capability to intelligently respond to this correspondence. Furthermore, so many of the proposals diverged significantly from anything we were remotely interested in supporting. Many foundations I've talked with that don't have a public presence complain of this overwhelming deluge of information, and more than one tells me that these proposals all quickly end up being shredded, unread.

When we went public, however, the reverse happened. The quantity of proposals we began to receive decreased, and at the same time, the quality began to increase. We began to receive intelligent and well-thought-out, strategic requests for our partnership. The result is that we now have a smooth system to handle the pressures of being the target of so many fundraising appeals. Our granting partners approve the majority of the completed applications we receive.

Openness benefits our charity partners, and even those charities that never become partners. Going public with lists of projects and charity partners allows all to see evidence of the types of projects that attract and sustain our attention. Some charities realize they can't compete with the field, and they refrain from applying if they have easier access to other money. Others step up their game and invest in developing projects that truly attract the attention of large donors.

Greater transparency is a way to live out our belief that all of us are gathered around a common table, contributing what we each have. Grantmakers contribute capital, influence, networks, and ideas. The charity partner contributes the necessary programs and its administration.

Another aspect in this maturing process in our journey of stewardship has been to be accessible and to engage with others. One of the consequences of increased visibility is increased pressures on our time, with requests for meetings, lunches, fundraising events, and the like.

Being transparent makes one vulnerable. But entities that have a considerable degree of power need to sacrifice the privileges frequently accorded the wealthy—the anonymity and the reluctance to be questioned—if they want to serve more wholeheartedly those they are helping. Through our transparency we are able to share information—good and bad—allowing others to learn from our experience.

Many charitable organizations find that potential givers—or even existing givers—build barriers to make themselves inaccessible. But playing hard to get is the opposite of what makes for effective philanthropy. Charities and donors both benefit from increasing accessibility. The charity benefits as a more robust, honest partnership can happen with a major donor. But philanthropists also benefit by understanding the wide spectrum of need and corresponding interventions on offer, and with experience can lean into their preferred solution.

Being accessible is a value that we believe we need to offer the social sector, and exploring ways to do that effectively is one of our strategic goals on an ongoing basis. We've explored various ways of becoming accessible over the years.

One unusual way of making ourselves accessible to charities in the past has been to do a road show where we meet face to face with several would-be applicants at once. Getting out and proactively addressing our philanthropic agenda creates significant good will within the community—simply by us making ourselves available.

In one instance, when we had a specific round of grants on offer, Brent and I ended up speaking in open meetings with more than a hundred organizational representatives over a two-week period in seven different Canadian cities, from Vancouver to Moncton. This was not only an efficient way to communicate our new partnership priorities, but it was intimate and inspiring too. We weren't the only ones with the floor: we asked organizations to share their own stories of transformational impact from around the world and heard stories of organizations that are reaching out beyond themselves to generously serve and offer hope in our world.

It's unusual for a foundation to be this accessible, and it can lead to some disappointment as certain charities recognize their programs are not at the core of what we are trying to accomplish. Others are excited as they realize the potential for partnership. But both groups are ultimately empowered by knowledge—even if their project isn't within our strategic framework, they know our position up front and this frees them to advance their cause with other potential partners. The nature of a transparent philanthropy ultimately improves accessibility to both current and potential partners.

Being readily accessible is possible only once you know your philanthropic priorities and your strategy for getting there, and then develop a system to anticipate the inevitable requests for participation. Defining this gives a platform from which to engage others; you don't need to feel defensive because the system you establish protects you. The reason for being accessible is that it allows you to communicate your message and granting priorities to others. It ultimately allows you to be more productive in your work.

As they become accessible, grantmakers can then engage as true participants with efforts that correspond to their interests. When we look at the stakeholders of a charity, funders are often mentioned but are seldom represented when program decisions are made. Being at the table allows for greater understanding by the charity in the passions that drive philanthropy. It also allows charities to begin to treat major donors as human beings and true participants in the work.

We find that once you become accessible, many may want your time and attention. It's not always productive to meet with everyone so we've developed ways to manage expectations and yet permit openness. For example, our current grantmaking partners have chosen not to fund smaller organization under a certain annual revenue threshold. This means that small agencies that would be overwhelmed by our larger-sized grants aren't eligible for our participation. We publish eligibility criteria for each round of grants, and request that organizations review these and ensure their eligibility prior to making appointments with us.

To manage appointments, as I said earlier, I've recently begun streamlining these basic inquiries into what I term "Charity Days," when I'm able to meet in fifty-minute segments throughout the day with eligible charity leaders, and quickly provide them with a sense of whether or not their organization and our partner foundations have common cause. This approach allows for a frank and honest discussion to find if there is convergence, and yet it doesn't overwhelm us as we are focused over the hour together.

I also ensure that I am present and accessible at events where people may want to make inquiries. For example, I typically attend the annual conference of the Canadian Council of Christian Charities and ensure I leave ample time for coffees with those who are interested in beginning a process with us. I also eat my share of chicken dinners each year at various fundraisers that seem to occur with intensity in late spring and late fall. Attending these galas allows for connections to be made both with other grantmakers and grantseekers.

Large-scale philanthropy can be a full time job if a grantmaker wants to be effective, but most of us don't have enough bandwidth to have personal interactions with every requesting organization.

Recognizing this, when my parents reorganized the assets of Bridgeway Foundation and created new foundations for the next generation as part of a succession strategy, I created a new organization. Stronger Philanthropy was designed to bring grantmakers and grantseekers together for greater impact. We manage the back offices of our family foundations, and our model of collaboration demonstrates that we can work together and provide greater impact through consolidating efforts with other grantmakers.

Another means to becoming accessible is a new initiative I am pioneering. The *Stronger Philanthropy Podcast* is a regular thirty-minute interview with fascinating grantmakers and grantseekers on major donor philanthropy. Our archive of interviews is large and growing, and becoming a much-appreciated resource for both grantmakers and grantseekers. Hearing real people talk about their giving is both inspiring and humanizing.

Attitudes

Conversations for your pilgrimage

1. What benefits and drawbacks would there be if you made yourself more accessible to those you are attempting to serve through grantmaking?

2. What measures could be developed to allow for a measure of accessibility while preserving some boundaries?

27

Patience required

Berducedo (Day 26)

I was one of the last to leave the albergue *this morning. This was uncharacteristic of me, but I had arranged to meet up with Léo who was camping on the road out of town, and I knew he was a late riser. His green tent emerged in the fog in a stand of trees as I approached; he was just packing up. I helped him roll up his tent, and we were off.*

Today a massive ascent awaited us. Within the first hour of walking, we stopped at a small café in Barras, the last stop before the climb. The server strongly recommended we phone ahead to make reservations as the cohort of pilgrims wanting to stay at the end of the stage today was much greater than the number of available beds. I tried calling but there was no answer. No matter: I was learning that the camino *would provide. We began climbing.*

Our ascent became the most spectacular day of walking I've ever experienced. Thankfully, the sun was out in full force; the sky was blue, and bluer still as we crept up the slope. We ascended to a peak of 1,100 meters, and most of the day walked along a cow path that traced a barren ridge above the tree line. The panoramic views in all directions revealed ten layers of mountains, each range a fainter indigo gray in the distance. In the foreground, the steep slopes were blanketed with purple heather, its color popping boldly against dried grasses.

We had been urged to carry our own food and water as throughout the day we were off the grid—there would be no cafés, no villages, nor even public fountains to fill a water bottle. Mine was full, and I had purchased an additional 1.5 liter bottle to resupply it; we also carried sufficient supplies for a midday picnic. After a considerable but rewarding effort we reached an abandoned stone albergue at the peak with spectacular views and enough shade by the wall to sit on the grass comfortably. We feasted on chorizo, cheese, baguettes, tuna pâté, spicy sardines in a tin, and red wine. It was a perfect, rejuvenating meal.

Following lunch, I discovered that my cell phone suddenly had reception—most of the day we had been out of range—so I called and reserved a bed at a private hostel. It was fortunate timing, as the owner told me I had secured the last available bed.

We continued apace, with more climbing, and then, suddenly, we faced a massive and precarious descent over loose shale. By three o'clock, we slid down the shale and reached a small village, really just a hamlet. Desperate for more water, we pleaded with the only resident we found to let us fill our bottles from her garden hose. At the far edge of the hamlet, we ran into Irene, Juan Manuel, and Juan Fernando, three Spanish pilgrims we recognized, sprawled out on the grass. We sat down with them to catch our breath; someone began telling jokes and soon we were all laughing hysterically—when you were this tired, everything became funny. We uncorked our remaining wine, and passed around the bottle. It wasn't elegant, but we were relaxed.

From this village, our maps told us we were still eight kilometers from our destination. Léo and I took off, and the sun beat down while we completed the remaining kilometers. We drank water thirstily, nearly emptying our bottles. Halfway there, we came to a slightly larger village with steep uphill streets. Climbing, we came across a Coca-Cola sign and red patio chairs—could it be a café? It was, but it was closed. We moved on, disappointed. Once again, we were desperate for water. Forging ahead, we covered the remaining distance, another hour, to Barceledo.

It was well after five when we finally arrived, having walked a full thirty-six kilometers and over the most rugged terrain we had yet experienced. Léo preferred to camp, so he set up outside town.

For two days I had been getting low on euros. Barceledo had no ATM, and the next available one was another day's walk distant. To my embarrassment, the inn wouldn't take credit. They were charging thirty-five euros for the room but I only had twenty-five in bills. When I explained my situation, Mabel, the owner, told me if I would take a roommate for the other bed, she would only charge us twenty-five each. Great deal for her! So when José Luis, a middle-aged Spanish walker arrived, we had a solution. All I had left were *seven euros in coins. My room situation had been resolved, but I sat outside the hostel on the porch, wondering how I could possibly afford dinner plus next day's breakfast and lunch before finding a cash machine.*

Once again, the camino *provided. Angel, the pilgrim from Madrid, lived up to his serendipitous name. As I sat pondering my options, he appeared and unexpectedly offered me dinner. Without me telling him of my financial predicament, he sat down and pulled out a full complement of chorizo, sardines, bread, and cheese, and insisted that I partake. Astonished, I gratefully and hungrily ate; this was like the loaves and fishes being multiplied in front of my eyes! Then, to my surprise—and this is when the story abruptly diverges from the biblical one—Angel pulled out a joint and smoked it.*

Urgent, unplanned giving is something we might do when our hearts are moved with compassion, or in response to a sudden tragedy. We instinctively give to crises. Our culture demands quick solutions, and philanthropy is no exception. We seek immediate change or begin to look elsewhere if there is a lack of apparent response.

In our pilgrimage of philanthropy, we needed to slow down, take time to learn more, and not react quickly. This more thoughtful approach to philanthropy requires us to familiarize ourselves with charitable operations, and to recognize that change of hearts and minds does not happen overnight. Most charitable passions—whether eliminating endemic disease in an impoverished economy, crafting and implementing solutions to homelessness, introducing spiritual value systems, or educating a new generation of creative thinkers—are works of art and soul, not works of technology or manufacturing. Adapting social mores and influencing cultural values is not as straightforward as crafting products for an assembly line or implementing multi-level marketing plans. Like walking across Spain, patience, perseverance, and a long-term perspective are required for substantive change to occur.

When we began to formalize our foundation operations, we went from funding general operating support with a blank-check approach based on our emotions to much greater definition and rigor around specific project-based funding. This was a necessary step in our learning. We needed to introduce accountability and precision to our granting. We wanted to measure tangible results. It was also a critical step for our partners in instituting discipline into their donor relationships. This was a helpful evolution for us, as we needed the boundaries that developed through a more thoughtful approach.

One day, a young man phoned me with a well-reasoned appeal to support his fledgling organization. Richard Taylor had recently graduated from university, and, with his business partner, Jeff Komant, had created the Wellspring Foundation for Education—a Rwanda-based entity seeking to elevate the quality of education beyond rote learning in the primary and secondary level education of Rwandan youth. I responded to Richard, outlining a few basic elements that, at the time, were the baseline for organizations applying to our foundation. While these may not be the criteria for everyone's philanthropy, they have proven to be a necessary framework for our success as a foundation. They included having charitable status, a minimum of $250,000 in annual revenue, two years' worth of audited financial statements, healthy board governance, and an innovative project.

Richard replied that the only thing he had on the list at that point was an innovative project that needed financing and one year's audited statements showing $150,000 in revenue. His board was just forming, and they had applied for, but had not yet received, their charitable status from the authorities. However, he vowed the criteria would one day be met. I wished him well, and hung up the phone.

The rationale for creating a minimum threshold for involvement assures us that, as a major donor, we are not left holding the bag for a small charity. Investing more than 10 percent of an organization's annual revenue through a grant creates an unfortunate reality where that one donor exercises undue influence, drawing rightful power away from the board of an organization. Healthy organizations have developed a donor base that spreads out the risk among a wider spectrum of donors both large and small. Determining the timing of involvement as an organization grows depends on the level of risk one wishes to take.

Surprisingly, Richard was back in my life a year later. He had taken my advice to heart, and had aggressively grown his organization to include what we considered essentials prior to getting involved. Since then, we have embarked on several creative projects with Wellspring Foundation for Education, projects that have maximized the potential of this small organization to influence the Rwandan educational system through teacher training and professional development.

My way of looking at this partnership has changed over time. While we consider grants as unique projects, bigger-picture thinking means that we take the long view and consider a series of projects to be an investment in more significant cultural change that is represented by the organization. In Wellspring's case, we have seen the Rwandan educational system being shaped through their strategic work, as the high caliber of their offerings means government agencies and other NGOs, both in Rwanda and now in neighboring countries, are coming to them wanting to partner.

I recently received an email from Wellspring's current CEO, Andy Harrington, notifying friends of Wellspring that he had received a call from the Minister for International Development requesting he meet with her in Ottawa. Normally, international development charities bend over backwards for years seeking large government grants, and rarely, if ever, would a meeting with the minister ever occur. However, due to Wellspring's growing reputation, they are now on the radar of Global Affairs Canada and an active partnership may soon emerge. This kind of impact can only come over many years of patient investment. Earlier investments are, even years later, still paying off.

Another example where we have made an investment of "patient capital" is that of Cardus. This Canadian think tank is rooted in a Christian worldview that sees that religious faith needs to positively contribute to the common good of society. Freedom of religion is coming under increasing suspicion within secular Canada, and liberties are being eroded; Cardus advocates for freedoms of all religions to practice their faiths, including when they engage in the public square.

As with all our grantees, Cardus approaches us on a project basis, developing time-bound and realistic projects that attract our funding. Specific projects we've supported have included investments into research, convening thought leaders, the development of publications, and capacity building. All have measurable objectives and Cardus has always excelled at reporting back to us on a timely basis. As important as project funding is, my greater interest lies in how, over time, the organization is consistently present to offer faith a place at the table in secular Canada. If they weren't there, who would be voicing this concern?

Because of the patient investing by Cardus' donors over the past decade and a half, President Michael Van Pelt has grown a small research organization with its origins in the labor movement into a wide-ranging and inclusive platform that explores the positive contribution religion can play in cities, work, economics, the family, healthcare, and education. They strategically acquired two similarly focused organizations, the Centre for Cultural Renewal, and the Institute for Marriage and Family Canada, enveloping these into its framework. They have opened an Ottawa office at the corner of Rideau and Wellington, just steps from Parliament Hill, to enable a more effective presence in lobbying government.

Funding research may seem to some to be tedious, or not sufficiently meaningful. But walking alongside Cardus over these past fifteen years has proven to be enriching as we witness the tireless work of Cardus's staff to promote a positive vision for faith in our society.

A final example of patient giving is in the area of the arts. Many philanthropists in my world are stymied by arts grants. How should one partner with artists in a meaningful way that ensures fruitful collaboration? Artists are not typically endowed with a results-based management mentality, and if that is the orientation of the grantmaker, there will be conflict. However, if the grantmaker embraces an attitude of patient investing, then over time, beauty may emerge.

For three years I learned firsthand these lessons as I participated on the board of *Image Journal*, a leading literary arts publication based in Seattle and founded by Gregory Wolfe. Much of their revenue was earned through the sale of the publication and events, but a quarter came through a patient, dedicated community of supporters that sowed into the belief that patient investing into the arts was worthwhile. Their annual Glen Workshop in Santa Fe, New Mexico was often a culmination point of grace and inspiration as aspiring and accomplished writers, dancers, sculptors, painters, filmmakers, actors, and poets gathered. They struggle with a faith that is often portrayed in our culture and preached in our pulpits as paint-by-number. Their struggle crosses boundaries and boldly paints outside the lines, with works of great beauty and worth emerging. One cannot invest in the arts with a quick, production mentality. Patrons must instead patiently walk alongside an artist, investing over the long term, investing in creativity. The results, though not quick or obvious, are frequently profound.

Conversations for your pilgrimage

1. In reviewing your past giving, is it characterized by emotional decisions or by a thoughtful approach and process?

2. What kinds of patient capital would attract your charitable investment?

28

Choosing to trust

Grandas de Salime (Day 27)

With seven euros jangling in my pocket, I tried to keep in mind the faithful provision of the night before. The albergue *didn't serve breakfast nor even coffee, so I pushed forward hoping for an open café somewhere along the route. All I had left in my bag of the previous day's picnic was a small stack of dried Melba toasts and water. At the first hamlet an hour outside of Berlucedo there were no services, so I sat at a picnic table and ate bread and water for breakfast.*

I continued on and summited a ridge with fantastic vistas. The camino *in this section followed the shoulder of the road, so I motored along, captivated by the spectacular view and missed a discreetly placed indicator showing the path branched off the road to the right. Twenty minutes later, after walking down the steep, paved road, I arrived in a small village. An older Asturian woman stood waiting for me in the street with a broom in her hand. "Are you walking the* camino?" *she asked me. "Sí, señora," I replied. "No, you're not," she retorted with a grin. She explained I would have to climb back to the top of the ridge, and take the proper path—the road I was now on would return me to where I had started earlier that morning. As I was low on water, I asked if she would mind filling my bottle, which she readily did from her laundry sink.*

Retracing my steps uphill, I finally found the right path and began an arduous and long descent through pine forests. Below me was a long, narrow reservoir, a finger lake created by the construction of a large dam. Despite my growling stomach, the walk was exceptional and transported me to British Columbia with the smell of pine, coupled with mountains and a lake.

I walked across the dam, and began ascending the opposite bank where I could see a café in the distance. This was my first opportunity at breakfast and coffee, and it was already noon. And, even better, on the patio on arrival, there was Léo chatting with Matthieu, another French pilgrim. I was ravenous, and ordered a bocadillo de tortilla *and large* café con leche. *But now I was down to two euros.*

I told Léo I wanted to keep pushing ahead, and kept moving onward alone. By three I arrived in the town of Grandas de Salime, walking under a banner that had been strung across the entrance of the community. It announced that today was a local fiesta *in honor of* San Salvador *(Saint Savior). I smiled: I had been saved. A few steps away, I found a bank machine and gratefully withdrew cash.*

The municipal hostel was packed to the gills, but the host showed me an overflow area—a dank basement garage crammed with bunk beds. A huge sliding steel door moaned and clattered when I tugged it open. I grabbed a bunk, had a shower, and began washing my clothes by hand. Once they were drying on the line, I took off for the center of town where once again, unexpectedly, Léo was sitting at a courtyard café with a few friends, Esben and Ben from Denmark and Matthieu from France. I pulled up a chair, and we stayed the rest of the afternoon enjoying the sun and conversation. After so many days of strenuous effort, these late afternoons were moments to truly relax and reenergize together.

In the evening, Léo, Matthieu, and I went into town for the fiesta. The whole town showed up and was buzzing with glee. Booming bursts from firecrackers announced the start of the party. Soon the band had set up, and a fast-paced salsa was playing loudly. The fiesta was like a magnet. We were drawn in, the park filled with the locals dancing. Among the crowd but standing off to the side were several pilgrims we had walked alongside for days. Since we didn't know their names, we had given them nicknames—the Viking (Teutonic, long blond hair in a ponytail) and the Punk (bearded Spanish guy with a nose ring). Along with them were several Spanish women pilgrims, so there were enough partners for everyone. We each grabbed a partner, and began shimmying to the salsa together.

At the beginning of our philanthropy, we took people at their word. We made significant grants based on verbal promises by charity leaders, based on annual visits made to our offices as they passed through Southwestern Ontario. As mentioned previously, with the scale of philanthropy we were attempting, this was not a helpful nor responsible position to take. If anything, this is an early stage in the philanthropy journey, one that quickly dissipates as experiences accumulate.

Once they have been burned a few times, philanthropists can find themselves harboring attitudes of jaded suspicion. I hear this in comments by others, and I know it when its ugliness appears in my own heart. This attitude can be manifested where there are unreasonable strings attached to the funding, leading to a place where the charity is hamstrung by donor intent. The basic assumption at work seems to be "we don't trust you to get it right, so you have to do it our way." But I wonder if we foundations really are the experts—or just the ones with money? Giving wisely means learning to trust those closer to the grassroots who have invested their lives into serving their clientele.

The underlying assumption behind this suspicion is that those with wealth know what's best for a charity. At times this assumption may have merit. Business skills and advice, management ability, and donor networks can all be contributed to enable better nonprofit work. But it is troubling when those with the money unduly influence the agenda of nonprofit operations. The money leads the conversation, not the earned expertise within the charity.

One organization we chose to trust was a controversial one. My friend Wendy Gritter has led New Direction Ministries for fifteen years. Wendy and I first met at the Evangelical Fellowship of Canada's Presidents' Day, an annual convening of ministry leaders, and soon became close friends. Hers was a small organization, barely big enough to qualify for our grants. But we respected Wendy's emphasis with her charity to create safe and welcoming spaces for LGBTQ Christians in churches. While she was leading in ways that were unconventional and occasionally made us uncomfortable, we chose trust rather than suspicion. It led to our sponsoring the development of a DVD resource called "Bridging the Gap" for church leaders and LGBTQ people of faith.

In time, Wendy led her organization down a painful yet necessary journey that was sadly interpreted by some of her donors. When she took over the organization as a freshly graduated ministry leader, it was an evangelical ministry that promoted the idea that a person could transition from gay to straight, and that this was the necessary path for gay Christians. As she listened and learned hundreds of stories firsthand, her doubts grew about the validity of reparative therapy. She eventually made a gutsy choice to publicly apologize and guide the ministry into one that advocated for what she termed "generous spaciousness" where people came before doctrinal positions, and people of faith could learn to hold in tension the divergent viewpoints within the community. Her book *Generous Spaciousness: Responding to Gay Christians in the Church*, outlines this position.

For a small organization rooted in an evangelical subculture, her decision made waves. Within a year, many large donors to her organization stopped giving, leading to a loss of 50 percent of donation income. People had to be laid off, programs reduced, and she retooled. The organization shrank so much that it was not large enough to qualify for our ongoing formal grants. But Karen and I continued to give on a personal basis, and are advocates for her efforts. Over time, and because of her perseverance and love for her community, it is clear to me she made the right choice. New Directions' international umbrella organization, Exodus, eventually followed her lead years later. Despite the trauma of her decision for the organization, New Direction is growing back organically, through the sustaining support of a growing, vibrant network of gay Christians throughout Canada, one that models grace, forgiveness, and inclusiveness.

Choosing to trust the on-the-ground implementer, rather than our own preconceived notions, was an important part of our own evolution as givers. For the philanthropist, trusting may mean making bold decisions to move your poker chips to the center of the table. It is risky to trust, but the rewards can be immeasurable.

Conversations for your pilgrimage

1. Which charities have you chosen to trust? Why?

2. Have you ever given despite misgivings and or with a level of uncertainty? What was the result?

29

Becoming responsive

A Fonsagrada (Day 28)

The dank overflow area of the hostel had become a sea of bodies scattered about. I awoke, and stepped over a mess of sleeping Italians who had crashed on every available square foot of floor. The massive door groaned on opening with an unearthly moan. With this racket, the Italians scurried to leave the premises, and they were far from quiet. The rest also woke up quickly, and one by one left.

I walked alone for a while, and soon came to a steep rise. I began climbing, but really, it was easier when done with the momentum of others. Strangely, but the very moment I thought, "I need someone to walk with," I turned around and there was Léo, climbing up the path. I paused to let him catch up and, once again, together we tackled the mountain.

Eventually we hit a final rise and crossed over from Asturias into Galicia, the last autonomous region of Spain we would enter. A row of rocks and a plaque etched on slate and propped up against the side of the hill announced our crossing into a Celtic land more linked to Brittany and Ireland than Castillian Spain.

After many hours, we ended in A Fonsagrada, a decent-sized town that was really the only stopping point for pilgrims today. The municipal albergue was completely full, so I found a private hostel. While more expensive, this hostel was an oasis with its fresh linens and corner room with rooftop views—a nice change from the previous evening.

I attended evening mass at the church around the corner. At the conclusion, the priest called forward the pilgrims and blessed them with a simple prayer. Standing alongside me were Luc and Dominique, a middle-aged French couple from Rennes I had passed earlier that day. They would hold hands as they slowly walked down the street. Their patient love was a reminder of the joys of a mature relationship, and it made me grateful for and miss Karen.

I then met up with Léo and Honor, a Dutchman, for dinner. Later, the Viking, a German we learned was named Julian, joined us. The evening ended with polemical discussion on Buddhist meditation and yoga with the Dutchman and the German holding widely divergent opinions. I found it humorously ironic that people could be so vehement when discussing meditation and nonviolence.

It's my conviction that, generally speaking, charities are the experts in social and spiritual change, not philanthropists. Many charity leaders have invested their lives into diverse subject matters such as homelessness, microfinance, food security, healthcare, theology, pastoral ministry, and the arts. The philanthropist, as a secondary member of the team, should direct energies into becoming responsive as an engaged partner with the charity.

The power of money exerts a force that is often hard to resist, and philanthropists can have a persuasive influence on charity life. But when money rather than expertise begins to set the agenda for charitable activity, we often see some odd contortions that are artificially contrived. Some grantmakers begin with an attitude of suspicion and often tightly attach strings to their grants that force charities to become brittle and inflexible in their operations. Others take the bull by the horns and show up with their minds already made up as to where funding should be applied.

My philanthropy journey has led me to discover a more flexible accountability, combined with transparent communication, that empowers charity leaders to do what they consider best, while at the same time keeping the donor fully informed.

When charity expertise and listening to the local context leads the way, we are witness to beautiful expressions of sustainability, respect, and impact. I think of our Stronger Together partnership with Toronto-based Sanctuary, a diverse community of people with various levels of material need, but including both wealthy Bay Street bankers and street-involved adults with challenging health issues and addictions. (The Bay Street bankers likely have their own addictions as well, though these are somewhat more acceptable and hidden in our society.)

As a charity, Sanctuary aspires to be a healthy community, not a program-based initiative to graduate the homeless into housing and employment. Certainly members of the community are encouraged towards meaningful work, but the organization doesn't make a program of it. In 2013 they approached our collaborative grants group, Stronger Together, to come alongside them in seed funding for a social purpose enterprise that would eventually offer full-time employment for a handful of community members. Toronto's United Way and others also invested seed capital for this initiative.

Switchback Cyclery was the result, a bike shop on Queen Street East in Toronto, that catered to trendy, build-it-yourself cyclists in the urban core. A few select members of Sanctuary's community were trained to be bike technicians; the bike shop is running a profit, and several full-time positions have been created. What is unusual is that Sanctuary has chosen not to "graduate" these individuals out of their jobs to find other jobs elsewhere. They believe that to offer a limited number of permanent, full-time careers will go deeper and last longer than rotating community members through a job training process. It also respected those community members who had finally arrived at a place of gainful employment.

Most grantmakers I know would take one look at this model and immediately want to turn it into a skills-training venture. We like outputs, seeing people trained, then moved forward into other careers. However, Sanctuary made a different call, one that was born from their expertise in walking alongside those who suffer with addictions and experience homelessness. Choosing not to push many people through a program but instead opening permanent employment for just a few was seen as the most appropriate solution for their community members who are usually treated as numbers or cogs in the social service machinery. Sanctuary's staff arrived at these choices only after two decades of learning, through many trials, errors of judgment, and painful reverses of fortune. As donors, we needed to respond to their earned expertise, not try to drive forward a new, more efficient model that had no context for this community.

Several years back, my wife Karen and I treated each other to a round of dance classes as an anniversary present. As left-footed beginners, we were learning the basics, and struggled to make sense of the cha-cha, the foxtrot, and yes, the salsa (which has come in handy). Week after week, we seemed to make only feeble progress. Finally, our instructor pulled us aside, and gave us a strict lecture. Both of us couldn't be leaders when we were whirling around the dance floor.

I'm happily married to a strong and decisive woman, but we soon learned that only one of us should lead. The other needed to relax and respond to subtle hand movements, the beat of the music, the twist of the hips, and the emotion on the face. Likewise, philanthropists must learn to soften our stance and become responsive to charities. As givers, we seek to empower them in their leadership of the social sector, and we willingly and joyfully glide along to their lead.

Conversations for your pilgrimage

1. What type of role do you exert as a philanthropist in relation to your charity partners?

2. Can you recall moments when you chose to follow the lead of your charity partner? What happened?

30

Nurturing accountability

Léo insisted on buying and making breakfast this morning, so I knew in advance we were going to have a late start to a long day of walking and surrendered my expectations. For this entire camino, eating on the fly, breakfast has been an unimaginative coffee and baguette toast, or, if I was lucky, a croissant. But Léo meandered to the grocery store, and when he returned, made eggs, bacon, and a tomato salad. I prepared the coffee. It was all deeply satisfying, but we were cooking in the communal albergue kitchen that was suddenly invaded by thirty-five Slovakian nuns on a camino bus tour.

The big breakfast and late start slowed us down. We slogged up and down the next ridges, heaving and sweating, feeling like we were moving through quicksand. At one point, Léo asked me which canister I had made the coffee from. "The small one," I replied. He began to laugh, "That was decaffeinated!" Now we knew why we were dragging.

The first open café finally emerged in the woods—a quirky place with sixties music playing. "C'mon baby, do the Locomotion with me" became an earworm, reverberating through my head for the next few hours. As we hummed along, Luc and Dominique showed up and we had a great connecting time and my French got a nice workout. Bolstered finally by two cups of real caffeine, we pushed ahead and now moved on quickly.

We had thought we were done with the big climbs. But there was one more significant one, and it was sheltered by trees, so we didn't see it coming. We ground our way up the slope, and were exhausted at the top, but kept pushing on. Another café in the path called us for another break. Finally, we arrived in O Cavado, a small Galician town in the hills. Léo secured the last cheap bed at the municipal albergue, *and, thanks to my phone, I had pre-reserved a spot at a private inn.*

Charities are often forced to blindly trust their donors. They gratefully receive any donations, and often develop expectations of annual contributions from their major partners. Donors often leave them hanging—the door is open a crack, an encouraging word is spoken, and expectations are fueled. But unfortunately the donor has not considered developing their own transparent process or communicating it clearly to the public. Greater accountability by grantmakers to their partners is a positive way forward.

The grantmaker offers a great service to charities when she considers her own limitations to partnership and communicates them clearly near the beginning of the relationship, or even better, on a website. She could define why they were partnering, how long it will last, the kinds of communication and contact expected, and how one will finish the granting partnership.

This begins in very simple ways. Grantmakers can consider adopting practices for themselves that include the basics of respect: returning phone calls, responding to emails, and stating one's priorities publicly. So much time would be saved by charities with clear, up-front communication.

Defining the terms of the partnership in an explicit manner will allow for freedom to exist in the relationship. Each party will know their roles and have realistic expectations of the other. Within these defined parameters, each is able to work harder, recognizing there is an end in sight and common goals to reach toward. As well, boundaries offer a sense of dignity to all parties. The terms have been stated, and an exit strategy has been articulated. The temptation for fundraisers to act like supplicants, always seeking the next potential grant, is reduced. The temptation for donors to become addicted to the feeling of being needed as fundraisers continue to woo them for more donations is likewise minimized. Healthy boundaries reduce codependency. If you're going to collaborate with respect, boundaries are essential.

At an annual Conference on Foundations conference regarding the need for donor accountability, Sean Stannard-Stockton, a columnist for *The Chronicle of Philanthropy*, made these observations:

> The most important message of the session and maybe the conference, is that transparency is not about public accountability, it is about improving the sector of philanthropy. It is about improving the way that all of us do our jobs. It is about transforming ourselves from a series of silos to an integrated, robust intellectual capital platform upon which all future grantmakers, big and small, can draw . . . .
>
> What philanthropy is engaged in is an experiment—an experiment in how we can all make the world a better place. We don't know what the right answer is. In fact, the "answer" is probably evolving as quickly as we can design experiments. But by being transparent, by sharing successful ideas and failed ideas. By judging ourselves not on the outcomes of each grant, but on the body of knowledge that we contribute to the field, we will truly transform philanthropy.[1]

The introduction of accountability for foundations is generally a foreign experience for many givers. Wealthy givers are not subject to market forces or accountability of any real kind; there are no real consequences for one's actions. If we deliver a "bad grant," there is no one to hold us accountable for doing so, and any feedback we receive from grantseekers is typically distorted—grantseekers have a vested interest in delivering good news to their funders. Any accountability by the grantmaker is one that is essentially self-imposed, and movements toward this will be highly respected within the social sector.

Like positive habits for healthy living—rigorous exercise and good nutrition—excellence in grantmaking is one that philanthropists will need to seek themselves. Foundations can create cultures for themselves which impose their own accountability and bring transparency to their processes. They could analyze our bottom quartile of grants, and learn from our granting failures. Grant recipients can be surveyed by discreet third parties hired to receive honest feedback, or to discover if we ourselves need to alter

1. Stannard-Stockton, "Impact," para. 9, 11.

our approach. One of the purposes of this book is to share not just our successes but some of our failures in the hopes that others will not have to tread the same dead ends we have trod.

Conversations for your pilgrimage

1. What kinds of accountability are important to you when seeking to give to charity partners?

2. How do you also make yourself accountable in your philanthropy?

31

Presence, the most generous gift

Lugo (Day 30)

Léo and I enjoy walking together, but he has limited resources and usually prefers to camp in a tent on the edge of town. Without discussing it, we have somehow slid into a morning routine where I leave early and walk ahead, but we end up connecting at some point later that day. We give each other autonomy and make no commitments, but it seems the camino *keeps pulling us together.*

Today was no different. While I walked in the pine forests, I paused to take my first picture of the day—a shot of the morning mists wafting through the trees, sun behind poking its head out of the fog. When I turned to continue on the journey, Léo had once again appeared on the path.

We walked in silence together for a while, then a small church appeared in the next village. Upon entering, I walked to the front and sat in a pew to reflect. I gazed upward, and suddenly knew why I was meant to be there. Before me, behind and above the altar, was a large carving of Santiago Matamoros. In most churches, Saint James is portrayed as a traveler, a pilgrim, who carries a staff and gourd for water. This time, unusually, he was depicted riding a horse, brandishing a large scimitar menacingly above demonic figures below him. Santiago Matamoros describes the legend of one who appeared to slay the Moors and gave victory back to Christian Spain after 800 years of Islamic rule. While it's a bloody, medieval image, to me it speaks of the power of God in bringing ultimate justice. It was a moment to release many years of an intractable situation that weighed heavily on me, where, despite my efforts seeking a restorative solution, ended with no communication and painful ambiguity.

As we exited the church, I decided to tell Léo this bitter story. He patiently listened and offered his support when, for a change, it was me doing most of the talking. The mantra of "let it go" continued to resound in my spirit, and I felt free.

We continued into Lugo, a fascinating Roman-founded city over 2,000 years old, and with massive, ancient walls surrounding it and architectural excavations through the downtown. We found lodging at a hostel, and after cleaning up ventured to the city center where we ran into some other pilgrims, saw the cathedral and Roman ruins, and ate a large, satisfying meal at a café on the street.

It's a normal reaction to want to avoid pain and suffering. We carefully craft our world so we are surrounded by maximum comfort and the illusion that all is well. The wealthier one is, the easier it is to create this artifice as money has the tendency to insulate the wealthy from the trials the majority face. But philanthropists who want to engage with the challenges of society can bravely learn from and follow their charity partners, surrendering aspects of the "good life" to enter into the reality lived by most of the world.

Perhaps this came easier to me than to many. For years Karen and I had lived in the developing world where we faced many daily examples of brutal poverty. The woman who came to clean our home when we lived in Bogotá was an example.

Dora was a single mother who endured a two-hour commute in cramped and inconvenient public transport a few times per week. We didn't know it at first but on days she worked with us, she was so desperately poor that she locked up her four-year-old and a one-year-old with a chain and padlock inside her simple wooden shack. She would leave behind powdered milk in bottles for the elder one to feed the baby. Several weeks passed until we discovered this shocking situation. It hadn't even occurred to us that she would abandon her kids to assist us. We eventually encouraged her to bring her children with her, a less-than-ideal solution, but one that would at least provide the little ones with supervision.

Dora wasn't our only shocking encounter with the misery of poverty. Several times a week, the pounding on our metal door brought me face-to-face with a man the neighbors crudely nicknamed Tangallo, literally meaning "Such a Rooster." Tangallo was intimidating: black filth covered his hands and face, the odorous reek of his unwashed, tattered garments was unbearable, and he was deaf-mute, communicating only through emphatic grunts and gestures. His mental capacity was impeded—his eyes would often wander to imaginary birds flying low, and he would yell and shake his fist at imaginary creatures that plagued him. He survived by collecting discarded bottles and cans in a large burlap sack, and returning them for recycling refunds.

We soon learned, however, that behind this frightening exterior, was a man whose face could shine with radiance. One early morning, we looked out the windows to view Tangallo stepping complicated tango moves down the street and around lamp posts, his arms carefully embracing an imaginary woman, the mournful, seven-step music playing only in his head. His demeanor also shifted dramatically with our toddlers present—peace would descend on him in the presence of children. There was so much more to Tangallo than met the eye or than he could possibly communicate. Although he was trapped within a body that was decaying, with a mind that distorted his reality, we learned to be present and to consider him a part of our daily life.

Tangallo would come to us for a hot meal. He intuitively knew when we would be cooking dinner, and we would always make extra for his meal, ready for when his invariable pounding hit our door. We would serve him his plate of food, and he would grin and grunt his pleasure. He sat on the retaining wall by our front door to eat, perhaps three or four times per week. When his bowl was empty, he would leave it politely on the stoop and disappear. Our neighbors began to complain that we were attracting this indigent to our street, but we ignored them.

Poverty was a daily reality on the streets of our city. When we took the bus downtown, we would be faced with many needier people than we could help: the disabled man with no legs, the woman with the football-sized goiter on her neck, the impish street kids who performed tricks for coins or who sold penny candy. We quickly realized we were never going to change the world. But we determined we would be selectively and consistently present in the lives of a few individuals, and avoided the shotgun approach to poverty. Like the singular starfish, we made a difference to one.

It was also an approach that urged us to come to grips with the reality and permanence of poverty. Whether poverty arrives through individual choices or from the (bad) luck of the birth lottery, we will always live with poverty in our midst. We are surrounded by inequity; we must learn to coexist by being present with grace and kindness for individuals entrapped in its injustices.

Closer to home, a bittersweet story was told to me by Linwood House Ministries. This was a small charity run by Gwen McVicker in Vancouver for fifteen years. Gwen modeled being present on the ragged edges of existence in the Downtown Eastside, Canada's poorest urban ghetto. She told me of her friend's story of a painful, not-always-successful journey towards hope—it wasn't a triumphal, sugar-coated victory parade like one we might see profiled on television. Her friend continued to be trapped by addictions and a lifestyle she wouldn't willingly select. She prostituted herself for dinner money. Yet what she came to understand—despite those unwanted appendages of addiction and lifestyle—was that she is a person loved by God and by a small coterie of women who make up Linwood's outreach. These simple relationships give her life, and provide slivers of hope despite her raw existence.

Philanthropists must learn that we can't fix everything. Despite compelling marketing campaigns touting the successes of nonprofit organizations, we never hear the whole story. Not everyone is restored to civic respectability and a life of meaningful contribution to society. Money and strategic interventions don't always repair the broken and wounded. I keep learning to be present with those on the margins, and to be patient in the midst of the messiness of life. Defying our fix-it mentality, we need to learn to live with the ambiguity of the human condition. I am learning that generous living does not always find tidy solutions; it must also learn to be present in unresolved pain.

Conversations for your pilgrimage

1. What are your limitations in philanthropy?

Attitudes

2. At what point are financial gifts irrelevant, and presence is a better option?

32

Granting dignity

Ponte Ferreira (Day 31)

Lugo was a fairly large city, and it took some time to exit it the next morning. But soon I ended up on a side road that went straight through the countryside past wheat fields and rolling hills. It was an easy but uninspiring walk, as it was mostly on a paved road where I had to watch for cars. It went on for hours and the first café of the day didn't appear until noon. I grabbed a sparkling water and rested, waiting for Léo to show up as he had done in the past.

Strangely, he didn't, so I carried on. A few kilometers later, another café appeared. It was fifty meters down a laneway hidden by trees, and not visible from the camino route, so I would miss Léo if he walked past. I was hungry and needed food. I devoured a bocadillo de queso. Just as I finished, Léo appeared. He was carrying his own stash of groceries, so launched into his own improvised meal.

Suddenly an English fellow also arrived, deeply struggling with the walk. The closer we got to Santiago, there were more new faces, and Ed was one of them. He had started walking the camino that morning in Lugo, and was full of questions and concerns; he was truly starting fresh. Ed was an English teacher in Madrid, and he lugged a too-heavy backpack and wore inappropriate footwear—he had no idea what to expect on this journey. He sat down with a groan, and kicked off his boots to examine inflamed blisters sprouting on his feet.

After resting up, eight more kilometers of walking eventually led us to a small village where Ed and I reserved bunks at a private albergue. Léo, once again, camped outside town, but he lingered with us, and we enjoyed chatting with the other pilgrims in the late afternoon sun. Later, the albergue held a community supper where we ate a fantastic seafood paella cooked in a meter-diameter pan over open flame. Over dinner, Ed and I shared the table with a mature Norwegian couple completing their sixth camino, something they do every summer, and two gutsy, elderly Australian women who were forces of nature with their brash talk and never-give-up attitudes.

A philanthropist who learns to be present has abandoned his self-protective reserve and the unseen walls that form a barrier between him and those being served. Wealth carries with it a series of expectations and distinctive cultural codes—from the way we dress to the language we use and the people we associate with. But to be present, one must drop the masks, be authentic, and, as much as possible, enter into another's life.

This was modeled for me most dramatically on a week-long sojourn in Ghana with Wayne Johnson, the former CEO of Opportunity International Canada. Their Ghanaian partner organization, Sinapi Aba Trust, graciously took us to communities across the country; each new trust bank that we visited held a ceremony of song, drumming, and dance when we arrived to hear their dreams. Millions of *cedis* (the Ghanaian currency) were currently being loaned out to 60,000 local clients. The investment Wayne was seeking from our foundation would leverage that further.

There was a buzz in the air among the staff as a particularly special visitor was soon to arrive near the end of our week. Baroness Janet Whitaker from the British House of Lords was scheduled to join us. She advocated for Opportunity International in the UK, and was on a tour of West Africa visiting various charitable organizations. As well, she was preparing to announce a specific investment which DFID, the British government's foreign aid agency, was making to the Ghanaian partner of Opportunity International.

The Ghanaian staff told us they were perplexed with how to prepare for the visit of a baroness. They had previously welcomed Princess Anne, who had traveled with an entourage of personnel under a well-managed schedule and clearly communicated set of expectations, but this Lady's office had sent no such instruction. Our own visit had offered us fantastic exposure to the entrepreneurial ability of the local people—but it had been a hot, sweaty, and exhausting experience. We breathed in enough diesel fumes and dust to turn our mucus black, we traipsed through markets filled with meager tables of moldy produce and raw cuts of meat covered with flies, and waited long hours in simple restaurants with stomachs growling for lunch to arrive. Wayne and I knew how to roll with the punches, adapting without complaint to the demanding circumstances. But I wondered how a baroness would fare under the same conditions.

On her arrival, we saw that the baroness obviously knew how to carry herself within the upper class British society. At the same time, I witnessed a beautiful adaptability in this woman. In each new context, she graciously abandoned the comforts of her class and stooped low to relate intimately to the poorest of Ghanaian women in the mud-walled hovels that were their homes. She held babies, hugged women, and listened patiently to simple stories translated from tribal languages.

After several hours of demanding travel and visiting, our hosts took us for a late lunch, but, as had already been our daily experience, we waited hours at the table for lunch to show up. By the time it came, we were ravenous. In this restaurant there was no menu—you ate whatever they served. When our lunches were plated, my eyes widened. I wondered how she would tackle this challenge: it was *fufu* and bush meat.

Fufu is the Ghanaian name for the staple throughout Africa—cassava pounded by hand into a sticky, starchy paste—and it lay congealing at the bottom of our soup bowls. Floating in each bowl were chunks of boiled bush meat—wild rodents or small animals hunted down in the jungle and sold by vendors who hawk their wares at the side of the road. The curved rib bones of a small mammal indicated it could have been rat, but we knew better than to ask. All this lay in the midst of a hot, watery tomato broth that had the pungent aroma of dried, smoked sardines. To top it all off, no utensils were provided. Our hosts blessed the food, and invited the baroness to begin eating.

Attitudes

Without a moment's hesitation, the woman who was accustomed to eat at white linen tablecloths with several courses worth of cutlery framing each plate, plunged her right hand into the hot soup and pulled out a long, stringy strand of fufu. Lips smacking, she ate, and we all dove in as well.

Sharing food may seem meaningless to the casual observer, but in this context, it meant everything to our hosts. What could have been the simple transfer of a million-pound grant by the UK government, was now shaded with great respect and admiration for one of the human faces behind the money. The baroness stooped low to relate to our Ghanaian partners—not only funds were given, but dignity was given through her gracious presence. She honoured her Ghanaian partners by abandoning her own comforts, and by eating together with them.

Perhaps dipping your hands in smoky soup in an African village is not up your alley. Our grantseeking partners still need grantmaker participation in other ways. One practical way to be present is by being named among the key supporters of a charitable effort. Being acknowledged as supporting an effort empowers the charity to fundraise more effectively with others when its key donors are listed.

One morning I found myself participating in a conference call with other major donors who were part of the Tyndale campus expansion campaign with its audacious fundraising goal. At times during the call, I felt myself recoiling—why am I doing fundraising? What strengths could I possibly offer this group? And yet, as I reflected on the nature of being present to others through philanthropy, I realized that assisting in this way was a natural way to leverage my presence to assist the institution.

That call resulted in my co-hosting an event where we invited those in our circle to hear about the new facilities. A select group of people responded and attended. We began with a meet-and-greet, lunch was provided, and the organization's leaders and I all offered perspective on this new endeavor. The lunch concluded with a quick tour of the new facility, which the school had proposed purchasing. Confidence began to build in other potential donors, and others soon joined us in contributing to this facility. Seeing participation by others after my own engagement brought me joy.

As we abandon our comfortable safety and vulnerably become present to the organization's mission, we enter into the essential practicalities of charity life. Chief among these is the need for fundraising. Confirmed donors provide an organization with the evidence that assists them in making their case for increased donations by others. A peer's commitment to financially sustain an organization is fuel to an organization's fundraising efforts among other potential major donors who respect what their colleagues have done.

When donors are drawn into fundraising for organizations, they cross a line. No longer are they objectively assessing from a distance, but they are proactively seeking others to support the cause. Their status as donor gives substantial weight to the organization's pitch—they themselves have financially invested and are willing to stand with the organization, offering their reputation and connections to the fundraising team.

Being present and participating makes us vulnerable. But in showing up, we participate with charities in more ways than just through our checkbooks. We enter into the challenges of organizational life, we experience both joyous and sad realities at the grassroots program delivery level, and we open our hearts to giving more than money.

It's easy to fall into the trap of treating major donors as little more than an ATM cash dispenser. You fill out a form correctly, punch some buttons, and out comes the cash. Worse, some givers view themselves in the same way. But philanthropy as transaction is reductionism at its worst. Understanding giving as a mere materialistic exchange forfeits its potential beauty where both giver and receiver are transformed through being present in relationship, united as they walk toward a common goal.

Conversations for your pilgrimage

1. In what ways have you chosen to be present in the situations where you give?

2. What has happened in others and in yourself in those decisions?

Transformation

It may be that when we no longer know what to do
we have come to our real work,
and that when we no longer know which way to go
we have come to our real journey.
The mind that is not baffled is not employed.
The impeded stream is the one that sings.

—Wendell Berry[1]

---

1. Berry, *Standing by Words*, 205.

33

An invitation to transformation

Arzúa (Day 32)

Today was the beginning of the end, and today everything changed. Our relatively untraveled and peaceful Camino Primitivo merged in the town of Melide with the Camino Francés, the most popular of all the Spanish caminos, as we joined paths en route to Santiago.

Sensing the upcoming change, our cohort of about twenty pilgrims who had most usually walked alone or in small groups began to coalesce as one. The impending deluge of people from other camino pathways subconsciously compelled us to draw together. Julian borrowed a ukulele from Guille, and played and sang as he walked, lifting our spirits with a compelling and haunting voice. I finally ended up chatting more in depth with the Spanish women I had danced salsa with several days earlier, and hooted with laughter when they revealed that for over a week now they had thought I was an Italian, not a Canadian.

As the caminos merged, our small wave of pilgrims that had become a family was suddenly overwhelmed with 500 or more people strung out along a crowded path. Some of these were those who had traveled the entire Camino Francés from the French border as I had done last year. But many, many more were those we dubbed "tourist pilgrims"; those who walked the required hundred kilometers from Sarria just to obtain the coveted compostela in the cathedral city. Most were vacationing groups of school kids, church groups, or neighborhood associations from the various corners of Spain and Italy, and their presence immediately changed the atmosphere. We went from contemplation to circus. Everybody walked faster, and raced for albergue beds that all seemed pre-reserved by these groups. Ed and I were grateful to eventually find a room in Arzúa, while Léo camped in the town behind us in Ribadiso.

After working with the predominant ATM cash dispenser model of philanthropy for some time—where it's simply a transaction with the donor providing money—it began to bother me. Something was wrong. Transactions made me feel reduced, not expanded. The philanthropy dance had become a commodification of the wealthy. We were commodities: we were traded on donor lists, and cropped up as names on buildings. We were no longer gifted collaborators, but cash dispensers. In our ongoing pilgrimage of philanthropy, we needed to migrate from this transactional philanthropy. But to what?

Henri Nouwen, an eminent Catholic theologian at Yale and Harvard, later abandoned his position and took up residence in L'Arche Daybreak north of Toronto with friends who suffered with extreme developmental disabilities. Despite his doctoral degrees and worldly experience, he became well aware of his own poverty, and through relationships at L'Arche he discovered a wealth he had not previously known. He invites the wealthy to a similar type of transformation in a brilliant booklet entitled *The Spirituality of Fund-Raising.*

Helping this booklet come into being was, for me, the best grant we never funded.

The Henri Nouwen Society approached us in the early 2000s to ask us to fund the publication of this small, unknown manuscript discovered after Nouwen's death in 1996. When I read it, I saw it contained pearls of wisdom that were much needed by both grantmakers and grantseekers. The society carefully put together a modest plan for publication, and our grantmaking committee reviewed their request for a fairly small but necessary grant. I had assumed we would quickly approve it, but in a strange turn of circumstances, our committee turned it down. I think, at the time, our group considered it to be too Catholic, too heady, and a little too far outside their comfort zone.

I was disheartened by this unexpected decision, but quickly recovered. I called up my friend Fritz Kling, the executive director of a foundation based in Richmond, Virginia whom I knew from our PIGS group. Fritz and I had had many conversations about philanthropy, and I knew this publication would greatly interest him and the grantmakers he worked for. After hearing my dilemma, he was very interested, and promised to present it to his board. Thankfully, within a few months, they approved it and the book was published.

What has happened since then is remarkable. This little piece of wisdom saw incredible success; it seemed to feed a hunger we all sensed but did not know how to satisfy. In the decade since its first publication, over 115,000 copies[1] have been distributed by Henri Nouwen Society, and it has become a much needed guide for grantseekers and grantmakers alike.

Nouwen sensitively but articulately describes the poverty faced by those trapped by this transactional philanthropy:

> Many rich people are very lonely. Many rich people suffer a lot from feelings of rejection or of being used, or of depression. And they all need a lot of attention and a lot of care. Just like the poor. Because they are as poor as the poor. And I want you to hear this, because so often I have come in touch with people who are totally imprisoned by thinking: "The only thing people see in me is money. So wherever I go, I am the rich aunt or the rich friend or the rich person, and I have these houses and these horses and these properties, and so I stay in my little circle, because as soon as I get out of it, people are there and say, 'he's rich!'"[2]

In our pilgrimage of philanthropy, we need to stop at the top of this mountain to take in the view and breathe in this important truth. We, who seem to have it all together and think we have a lot to contribute to the world, in reality, are poor. We are needy. We don't have it all together. We are isolated. We need community. We need to learn to receive, not just give.

Those who receive our funds are actually very wealthy in many ways we are not. We have much to receive from them, if only we will open our

---

1. Email with Karen Pascal, executive director, Henri Nouwen Society, March 4, 2016.
2. Nouwen, *Spirituality of Fund-Raising*, 18.

hands, not only to give but to receive. When we recognize the wealth they have to share with us, we confer to them dignity.

Doing philanthropy without being willing to be changed ourselves is not adequate, and really defeats the purpose of giving. Giving is not about the gift, but about the giver engaging and becoming part of the community. Giving is about being changed oneself. We need to get our eyes off the financial transaction, and onto the transformation of the heart.

In a similar vein but with a different voice, Rwandan President Paul Kagame provides a clear perspective about how the wealthy West has much to gain by investing in and participating alongside Africans in our ongoing mutual development. It's not just about the Africans' or Latin Americans' or Asians' need. It's also about our own need to be in community, to be jarred by the realities of life.

Kagame begins by affirming participation by Westerners in his country's development, but then adds that they also will receive much by entering into and learning from Rwandan culture and life:

> [Westerners] are well educated, optimistic, and keen to assist us as we continue to rebuild, but one must also recognize that we have much to offer them as well.

> We will, for instance, show them our system of community justice, called *gacaca*, where we integrated our need for nationwide reconciliation with our ancient tradition of clemency, and where violators are allowed to reassume their lives by proclaiming their crimes to their neighbors, and asking for forgiveness . . . .

> We will show your sons and daughters our civic tradition of *umuganda*, where one day a month, citizens, including myself, congregate in the fields to weed, clean our streets, and build homes for the needy.

> We will teach your children to prepare and enjoy our foods and speak our language. We will invite them to our weddings and funerals, and out into the communities to observe our traditions. We will teach them that in Africa, family is a broad and all-encompassing concept, and that an entire generation treats the next as its own children.

> And we will have discussions in the restaurants, and debates in our staff rooms and classrooms where we will learn from one another: What is the nature of prosperity? Is it subsoil assets, location and sunshine, or is it based on human initiative, the productivity of

our firms, the foresight of our entrepreneurs? What is a cohesive society, and how can we strengthen it? How can we improve tolerance and build a common vision between people who perceive differences in one another, increase civic engagement, interpersonal trust, and self-esteem? How does a nation recognize and develop the leaders of future generations? What is the relationship between humans and the earth? And how are we to meet our needs while revering the earth as the womb of humankind? These are the questions of our time.[3]

Both Nouwen and Kagame, in their own unique ways, offer us a similar challenge. Their view of the human community includes all people, and all are needed. Both grantmaker and grantseeker can drop the roles we are frequently forced into, and learn to be present to one another as human beings. To rise to this challenge will mean to become vulnerable, and open ourselves up to the opportunity to be transformed.

Conversations for your pilgrimage

1. Can you identify with Nouwen's perspective of being trapped by transactional philanthropy? What has led to this?

2. How can you enter into community to be transformed?

3. Kagame, "About Aid," para. 4–8.

34

Transformed by philanthropy

Monte do Gozo (Day 33)

The tourist invasion of new pilgrims on the path was a shock after weeks of walking in quiet contemplation, and it reminded us that our arrival in Santiago was imminent. Though surrounded by crowds, our small camino *family began withdrawing, going silent, mentally preparing for arrival at our destination.*

The Way now gently curved, hundreds of thousands of boots and poles had carved a deep, broad, rounded path through the forests and fields. Shining bars and cafés sprouted like mushrooms every other kilometer, and long lines for service were a stark contrast to the previous weeks of solitude and inward contemplation.

I walked with our new friend, Ed. His plan was not to stop in Santiago, but to move on through to Finisterre, the town on the edge of the Atlantic three days' walk beyond Santiago. He had no religious leanings, nevertheless, the camino *began to work its magic on him as well. As we talked, he said he was astonished he hadn't met anyone from the UK. The very moment the words flew out of his mouth, we happened to be walking by a man repairing a fence at the side of the road. We greeted him, and he responded with an English accent. It turned out he was an Englishman who had a transformative experience walking the* camino, *and had just purchased the property he was fixing up. He lifted up his shirt to reveal a full torso tattoo of a map of the* camino *to prove his point.*

After thirty-nine grueling kilometers in the hot sun, Ed and I arrived at Monte do Gozo, the last albergue on the camino to Santiago, and which overlooked the cathedral city itself. For over a thousand years, pilgrims had stood in this place and seen their destination for the first time. Once again, at this lookout, we ran into Léo, and soon other Primitivo pilgrims we knew began arriving, too: Julian, Dani, Anna, Aubrey, Ben, Esben, Beatriz, Irene, Juan Fernando, Juan Manuel, and other familiar faces. We were overwhelmed by the much larger contingents from the other caminos.

Spontaneously, we decided to cook a last communal meal together in the albergue kitchen, each one contributing pasta, vegetables, chorizo, or wine. The shared kitchen space was a madhouse. Seven cooks were at work with too few pots and too few plates. An ambitious Spanish woman cooking for a youth group had prepared too many meatballs, so she generously added many heaping spoonfuls into our humble pasta. Due to the crowds, there was no room left inside, so our group moved outside. We sat on the ground in a circle, eating from a communal pasta pot and drinking Rioja from teacups. Some Spanish kids who were walking the camino approached us and asked if they could sing some of their songs for us, and soon we were singing with abandon accompanied by a simple ukulele. It was the perfect final evening on the camino.

In our own philanthropy journey, we have been humbled, shattered, overjoyed, and blessed by participating with others who are unlike ourselves and who offer very different gifts.

My friendship with Noel Hutchinson from Asian Outreach Canada began during my years at Bridgeway. In early 2011 he invited me to join him on a scouting mission in Northeast Cambodia where he was investigating the potential to develop holistic outreach for rural villagers. His invitation was precipitated by an impending event. The neglected province of Stung Treng in the Greater Mekong Subregion was designated by the Asian Development Bank and ASEAN governments to become the locus for an east-west highway linking Thailand to Vietnam's coast, and a north-south axis joining China's Yunnan province and Laos with Phnom Penh and Cambodia's southern coast. Within years, rural villagers would live at a crossroads for mega-Chinese investment, creating opportunity but also greater likelihood for human trafficking and exploitation.

Our small group hopped on motorcycles, crossing the Mekong River in a wooden boat with our bikes balancing precariously in the stern. Upon docking, we dove into the jungle. We rode paths barely fit for walking, but which linked remote village communities. In two days we covered 380 kilometers and, as a novice biker, I had the ungainly misfortune of wiping out eighteen times. I ate dirt and smashed up my legs many times that day, but I kept picking up that heavy bike and persevering.

We met villagers who lived a subsistence life, who barely lived on rice and the morning glory vegetable they grew. Money was almost unknown, as families would rarely venture beyond their small region and bartering with neighbors for goods was the only type of transaction known. In their poverty, most families had sent sons and daughters to Phnom Penh, Bangkok, or Kuala Lumpur to work. These young, at-risk teens were often exploited for their labor or the sexual services they offered. Sicknesses and misery abounded; it was truly tragic to witness.

Under the direction of Noel's colleague, Thong Romanea, executive director of Asian Outreach Cambodia, a plan emerged to begin to create options for a sustainable future within this rural region, as well as the immediate response to some more pressing needs. This meant an agricultural solution was required. The solution was devised in the minds of Cambodians for Cambodians.

Over the next five years, Noel took the lead in raising funds for the creation of an agricultural training center and farmers' cooperative which was eventually sponsored by Bridgeway Foundation, Stronger Together 2014, Charis Foundation, Acts of Grace Foundation, and other generous Canadians, Kiwis, Singaporeans, and residents of Hong Kong. As I write in early 2016, I have just come from the dedication of the center which I attended with Karen, my sons, Daniel and Nate, and Daniel's wife, Andrea. It was the first time my adult children had visited Cambodia, though in this past half-decade, Karen and I have grown increasingly committed to this place and have visited over a half-dozen times.

Asian Outreach now offers support and services in twenty-six villages of Stung Treng, including the provision of water filters and latrines, agricultural training, health care education, and early childhood education. Their fifteen local Cambodian staff liaise with governments and advocate for social improvements. The organization believes their new agricultural training center and model farm will begin to staunch the flow of youth to the cities as sustainable livelihoods are within reach.

Earlier that day we had seen samples from the model farm—cashews grown as a lucrative crop, odorless pig pens, hydroponic gardens, mushrooms multiplying under moist rice hay, stocked fish farms with henhouses sitting overhead, supplying the water with rich nutrients. I was drawn to the mango tree saplings growing in the nursery. Staff showed us how a mango branch from a species known to produce many mangoes annually had been grafted into another one from one that produced fewer mangoes but more frequently, at two crops per year. The hope was that through the melding of their strengths a new species could be developed that was even more fruitful.

I stood beside Romanea in front of invited guests at the dedication; he translated my words into Khmer. I described how we were brothers. We didn't look like brothers—I'm a white guy and Romanea is a rich, caramel hue, but we've been grafted into the same family of God, as we are all God's children. Like the mango trees that were being grafted together, we too were being bound as one, and as a result could be more fruitful together.

As two distinct mango branches are united, a transformation begins to occur. In like manner, our transformation is happening as well. Karen's frequent visits to this country, and walking alongside female Cambodian NGO leaders in a mentoring capacity, have changed her as well as them. A transformation is also occurring in me, as I walk alongside and hear the stories of resilient Cambodians who have suffered traumas from the Pol Pot genocide and the Killing Fields that minimize anything I've ever faced.

This has also impacted the way we give. Transformational philanthropy takes the risk of abandoning our carefully curated worlds, flinging open our doors, and willingly engaging with those with whom we are on the journey. It becomes a pilgrimage, a road on which we boldly walk, willing to be transformed by the often daunting journey.

Transformation

Conversations for your pilgrimage

1. In what ways is your philanthropy transformational—not only for others, but for yourself?

2. Who can accompany you on your pilgrimage of philanthropy?

35

A philanthropy on pilgrimage

Santiago de Compostela (Day 34)

Léo and I had decided several days ago that we wanted to walk into the city together. Early on in the Primitivo journey, he had shared stories of his early childhood that wrenched my heart. His father had tragically died when he was eight, and he was forever impacted by that loss.

It was hard to comprehend this kind of pain for a child, and he was walking it out all the way from Mont-St-Michel. I didn't have much, but gave what I could: my own presence as a dad who cheered him on to the finish. By walking together through pain, hunger, and exhaustion, I couldn't offer much more than accompaniment. It seemed as if the camino wanted us to walk together—so perhaps our journey together was meant to be.

Today's walk was only five kilometers through the outskirts of the city, with modern structures and broad boulevards gradually giving way to the old town with its narrow streets and tall buildings that encroached on the path and seemed to push us forward. These restrictive passageways became a birth canal; pressure was building, and we were about to arrive. We followed arrows through one final archway, a Galician bagpiper sounding a mournful wail, and the camino gave one last, desperate push like a woman giving birth. We emerged blinking and newly born into the plaza in front of Santiago's cathedral.

We collapsed on the pavement and watched others arrive. Each new arrival responded differently. Some wept in joy. Others did a happy dance. Others fell to their knees, while some sprawled on the ground and lay there for hours to drink in the moment. Everyone took selfies with the cathedral behind them, and photos of those they had journeyed with.

Though we hadn't seen her for about ten days, suddenly there was Katjuša leaping over to us with a grin on her face. We embraced with joy, and later, we went for dinner together. A few hours later, as I walked the crowded streets of the old city, I turned a corner and literally bumped into Jaffer! We arranged to meet up for one last lunch and to hear the stories of each other's camino journeys since we had parted ways.

But the culmination of this pilgrimage was the cathedral. I wanted time to pray alone in the gracious building; perhaps I would see the massive bota-fumeiro dramatically swinging with clouds of incense across the length of the transept, the distance of a football field, and pulled with the strength of six monks.

On entering, I saw a small notice mentioning a daily morning mass in English in a side chapel, and so I sought out a chance to commune with God in my own language with a small group of fifteen other pilgrims. An Irish priest presided over the Eucharistic meal.

There are some physical places on Earth where God seems especially near—the Celts used to call these thin spaces. With the thin space of the camino, God had come near, and here at its climax, he did so once again. In a strange twist of events that I could never have planned, our arrival day happened to be August tenth, the Feast of Saint Lawrence. As a result, Lawrence's life and martyrdom was highlighted during the mass.

Lawrence, a Spaniard from Aragón, had been a deacon in the church in Rome during a time of great persecution in 258 AD. When the pope was taken away for execution, he handed the keys of the treasury to the deacon for safekeeping. He prophesied that Lawrence would follow him to an early death in three days' time. Shrewdly, Lawrence took the wealth of the church, and distributed it to needy peasants and beggars in the city's piazza. Three days later, as predicted, the Romans arrived to seize him; they wanted the money. Instead, Lawrence opened the doors of the church, revealing the homeless of the city at the doorstep, and saying, "These are the wealth of the church." The Romans wanted transaction; Lawrence gave them transformation.

Furiously, they dragged Lawrence to an open fire, and chained him to a grill for his execution by fire. While dying, he famously commented with wry humor, "Turn me over, the other side isn't done yet." On August tenth each year, an appropriate (if macabre) way to honor him is to hold a barbeque for your neighbors.

Lawrence's last days sealed the story of a man who had an upside-down perspective of reality that contrasts with society's normal mode of seeing life. The value of each human life, and in particular the poor, is filled with promise. His actions teach us that financial wealth is bequeathed to us for sharing, and is not for selfish gain or promotion.

Over twelve years earlier, when I wondered who could be a model for my philanthropy, I discovered this story of Saint Lawrence and adopted him as my inspiration. And here I was today walking into Santiago on his feast day. Lawrence is a patron saint for philanthropy, as well as humor and feasting, each one a mark of true community. His story marked the end of my camino. And it begins my onward journey as well.

In our philanthropic journey, we started with heartfelt but somewhat naïve assumptions. We gave independently and reactively. Over time, we learned to channel resources towards innovation and capacity building. We learned to drop our barriers and found ways to meaningfully engage with our charitable partners. We learned that giving for impact will never happen quickly, and we must patiently watch the changes occur over years. We also learned that giving in isolation means duplication of effort and giving at cross-purposes with others. Instead, greater communication produced efficiencies, and giving together multiplied results.

This philanthropy pilgrimage moved us away from a transactional perspective regarding wealth. Charities need the practical, financial means to implement their visions. Grantmakers must develop ways to wisely steward their resources. But giving is not just about a financial transaction. Our giving can lead to transformation of ourselves and of others.

Remember the story of the woman who gave all she had to the temple treasury? Two small coins, enough for just one loaf of bread. One hundred percent of her savings. It was an insignificant gift that was essentially meaningless when viewed as a transaction. Others were applauded for their larger donations, and the woman forgotten. But when she gave her all, Jesus reminded us that this woman, not the others, was to be remembered.

In giving all that she had to live on, even a day's ration of bread, she surrendered and trusted God to provide. The transformation that occurred by having the faith to surrender it all is a model we can learn from. This kind of humble faith is what will ultimately endure.

I'd like to share one final story, a post-resurrection account of two men walking home to their village of Emmaus. They too were on pilgrimage: a journey away from the disillusionment and pain of the crucifixion of their friend. They thought they had found their Messiah, the one who would bring his new kingdom to Israel and end the oppressive Roman regime. But what they supposed was the answer to their oppression had died. Their dream of a new way of living had been snuffed out with the gruesome death of their leader.

Little did they realize that as they walked their *camino*, they would be transformed by an encounter with an unknown stranger. Their hearts burned as they discussed the incomprehensible events of the past few days, but as they ate bread and drank wine together, their eyes were opened to recognize Jesus himself had joined them at the table. This sacramental moment reveals a beautiful truth: it is as we journey together that we become open to new ways of viewing life, new forms of discovering abundance. There's something about movement away from the known and the secure that enables us to drop our guards and consider new ways ahead.

Most of us who have any potential in giving have plenty to live on. It is much easier to hold back and to refrain from giving, or to give but not to engage. But a decision to hold back is a choice that impoverishes all of us. Giving means letting go with great generosity. We give with open hearts and minds and hands. We give in relationship, yet always protected by appropriate boundaries. We give freely, but thoughtfully, carefully, and strategically. As we walk this philanthropy journey together, we grow to discover many of our charity partner friends truly are giving their all in service, in love, and in generosity. We are all changed as we walk together.

> So we saunter toward the Holy Land; till one day the sun shall shine more brightly than ever he has done, shall perchance shine into our minds and hearts, and light up our whole lives with a great awakening light, so warm and serene and golden as on a bank-side in Autumn.[1]

1. Thoreau, "Walking," para. 26.

Conversations for your pilgrimage

1. Who walks with you on your pilgrimage?

2. How will this walk change you going forward?

Acknowledgements

My gratitude is extended to many people who have journeyed with me over these past years, and who have had a part in seeing this book come to fruition. I began writing one summer sitting on the edge of a volcanic lake in San Marcos, Guatemala, not being satisfied and shelving the manuscript for a few years, and resurrecting the book only once the metaphor of pilgrimage began to emerge.

There are people who prayed, supported, loved, and believed on this journey. Thank you Greg and Andrea Pennoyer, Chris Orme and Melinda Estabrooks, Marie MacNeill, Norm Allen, David Stiller, John McAuley, Fr. Neil Macmillan, John Scerri, Ken and Luella Hillmer, Judy and Dennis Shierman, Ruth and Bob Coghill, Alma Petersen, Stephen and Beth Lauer, Emily Enns, Fred Smith, Todd and Karen Hendricks, Aaron LeClaire, Jeremy Floyd, Helen Sworn, Chris and Phileena Heuertz, Brent Fearon, Randy and Nadine Mitchell, Alexandra Horwood, Wendy Gritter, Rick Tobias, Lorna Dueck, Iris Armstrong, Simona Ilieva, Janis Ryder, Anna Marie White, Doris Olafsen, Martha Arias, Jim Frantz, Gilberto Rubio and Martha Bernal de Rubio, Hermana Patricia, John Pellowe, Rod and Bev Wilson, Gary Nelson, Darrel and Barb Reid, Glenn Smith, Linda Milke, Nery Duarte, and Wayne Johnson. There are many more unnamed family and friends who have whispered a prayer or who have walked alongside; I am grateful for each one of you.

I am also grateful for others:

To faithful companions I met and walked with on the *camino* journey in 2015, including Jaffer Syed, Léo Del Torre, and Katjuša Gorela.

To our Stronger Together grantmaking group, but especially John and Rebecca Horwood who consistently cheered me on and celebrated as we leveraged our giving to the max.

Acknowledgements

To my diligent friend and colleague, Linda Dzelme. I can't imagine accomplishing anything without your confidence and support.

To my editor, Rodney Clapp, and the team at Cascade Books, who helped birth this baby into existence and took a leap of faith with an unknown author. Susan Fish of Story Well provided me with creative suggestions and a first edit. Others graciously provided perspective and feedback on beta versions of this book, including Kie Naidoo, Davis Mitchell, and Larry Matthews.

To my extended family, including the visionary founders of Bridgeway Foundation, my beloved parents, Reg and Carol Petersen. To my brother, Mike, and his wife, Kim Petersen, who generously gave of themselves so our family philanthropy could be sustained over the long term. And to my sisters and their husbands, Shari and Paul Reid, Amy and Tony Campbell, and Melissa and Lee Carter.

Finally, to my sons Daniel and Nate, and Daniel's wife Andrea, who have each offered unflinching support and endless love. I'm proud of who you have each become as young adults, and I will never forget that moment together on our rooftop in Cartagena. As the sun was setting over the Caribbean, eternity was condensed into a moment.

Most of all, my gratitude and love goes to my soul mate of twenty-seven years, Karen Petersen. Together we keep exploring the world—not only walking Spanish *caminos*, but also riding Chinese railcars, Bolivian buses, Filipino jeepneys, Vietnamese junks, Italian catamarans, Cambodian tuktuks, Icelandic whalers, Colombian taxis, and Canadian canoes. We are on a lifetime of pilgrimage, and one day we will stumble forward together into the new Jerusalem.

–Feast of Pentecost, May 15, 2016

Learn more about Stronger Philanthropy

Stronger Philanthropy multiplies impact for grantmakers. We leverage donations by granting together. We offer streamlined systems, clear communication, worry-free administration, and accountable partnerships with charities.

For more information on our work and to discuss possibilities for partnership, visit our website at www.strongerphilanthropy.ca.

Bibliography

Anheier, Helmut K., and Diana Leat. *Creative Philanthropy: Toward a New Philanthropy for the Twenty-First Century.* New York: Taylor and Francis, 2006.

Berry, Wendell. *Jayber Crow.* Berkeley, CA: Counterpoint, 2000.

———. *Standing By Words: Essays.* San Francisco: North Point, 1983.

Boers, Arthur Paul. *The Way is Made by Walking: A Pilgrimage Along the Camino de Santiago.* Downers Grove, IL: InterVarsity, 2007.

Bolduc, Kevin, et al. *Beyond the Rhetoric: Foundation Strategy.* Cambridge, MA: The Center for Effective Philanthropy, 2007.

Bravo, Nino. "Un Beso y una Flor," 1972. http://www.musica.com/letras.asp?letra=904953.

Brierley, John. *A Pilgrim's Guide to the Camino de Santiago: St. Jean, Roncesvalles, Santiago.* Forres, Scotland: Findhorn, 2015.

Connolly, Paul, and Carol Lukas. *Strengthening Nonprofit Performance: A Funder's Guide to Capacity Building.* Saint Paul, MN: Amherst H. Wilder Foundation, 2002.

Corbett, Steve, and Brian Fikkert. *When Helping Hurts: How to Alleviate Poverty Without Hurting the Poor and Yourself.* Chicago: Moody, 2009.

Council on Foundations. *Best Practices in Grants Management.* Washington, DC: Council on Foundations, 2001.

Fleishman, Joel L. *The Foundation—A Great American Secret: How Private Wealth is Changing the World.* New York: Perseus, 2007.

Frumkin, Peter. *The Essence of Strategic Giving: A Practical Guide for Donors and Fundraisers.* Chicago: University of Chicago Press, 2006.

Gillet, Kit. "Cambodia Trains Social Workers to Curb Reliance on Foreign Aid." *The New York Times,* June 18, 2013. http://www.nytimes.com/2013/06/19/world/asia/19iht-educside17.html?_r=0.

Harman, Leslie D., Editor. *A Sociology of Pilgrimage: Embodiment, Identity, Transformation.* London, Ontario: Ursus, 2014.

Heuertz, Phileena. *Pilgrimage of a Soul.* Downers Grove, IL: InterVarsity, 2010.

Jeavons, Thomas H., and Rebekah Burch Basinger. *Growing Givers' Hearts: Treating Fundraising as Ministry.* New York: Jossey-Bass, 2000.

Kagame, Paul. "A Different Discussion About Aid." *Huffington Post,* July 10, 2009. http://www.huffingtonpost.com/pres-paul-kagame/a-different-discussion-ab_b_213370.html.

Karnofsky, Holden. "The Case Against Disaster Relief." http://blog.givewell.org/2008/08/29/the-case-against-disaster-relief.

Bibliography

Lerner, Michael. *A Gift Observed: Essays on Philanthropy and Civilization*. Bolenas, CA: Common Knowledge, 2005.

Lupton, Robert D. *Toxic Charity: How Churches and Charities Hurt Those They Help (And How To Reverse It)*. New York: HarperCollins, 2011.

Machado, Antonio. "Proverbios y cantares XXIX." *Campos de Castilla* (1912). https://es.wikisource.org/wiki/Proverbios_y_cantares_(Campos_de_Castilla).

Norris, Kathleen. *The Cloister Walk*. New York: Riverhead, 1997.

Nouwen, Henri J. M. *The Spirituality of Fundraising*. Nashville: Upper Room, 2011.

Orosz, Joel J. *Effective Foundation Management: 14 Challenges for Philanthropic Leadership*. Lanham, MD: Alta Mira, 2007.

———. *The Insider's Guide to Grantmaking : How Foundations Find, Fund, and Manage Effective Programs*. San Francisco: Jossey-Bass, 2000.

Prashad, Sharda. "Compensation: Pursuit of Happiness." *Canadian Business*, September 15, 2008. http://www.canadianbusiness.com/business-strategy/compensation-pursuit-of-happiness.

Rooney, Patrick, and Heidi K. Frederick. "Paying for Overhead: A Study of the Impact of Foundations' Overhead Payment Policies on Educational and Human Service Organizations." Unpublished working paper. Indianapolis: The Center on Philanthropy at Indiana University, March 2007.

Rowell, John. *To Give or Not to Give? Rethinking Dependency, Restoring Generosity, and Redefining Sustainability*. Tyrone, GA: Authentic, 2006.

Shaw, Luci. *Harvesting Fog*. Montrose, CO: Pinyon, 2010.

Stannard-Stockton, Sean. "Demonstrating Impact: Philanthropy's Urgent Call to Action." *Tactical Philanthropy Blog*, June 29, 2007. http://www.tacticalphilanthropy.com/2007/06/demonstrating-impact-philanthropy%E2%80%99s-urgent-call-to-action-2.

———. "Grant Makers' Fiduciary Duty Should Extend to Grantees." *The Chronicle of Philanthropy*, June 13, 2010. https://philanthropy.com/article/Fiduciary-Duty-at-Foundations/160513.

Thoreau, Henry David. "Walking—Part 3 of 3." *The Thoreau Reader*. 1862. http://thoreau.eserver.org/walking3.html.

Walsh, Peter. *It's All Too Much: An Easy Plan For Living a Richer Life With Less Stuff*. New York: Free Press, 2007.

Wilhelm, Ian. "Canadian Family Pioneers Guerrilla Giving." *The Chronicle of Philanthropy*, October 23, 2009. https://philanthropy.com/article/Canadian-Family-Pioneers/193557.